and
Tenacity

Women Transforming Leadership in Business and Community

Curated by Cathy Derksen

ISBN: 978-1-962825-34-4

Powered By

C-SUITE NETWORK

Foreword

As leaders, we are no strangers to the unique challenges and extraordinary opportunities that come with stepping into our power. In this book, Cathy Derksen masterfully captures the essence of what it means to lead with authenticity, resilience, and a relentless drive for impact.

This read is more than just a collection of stories; it's a testament to the strength and courage of women who have refused to let obstacles define their journey. Cathy has woven together narratives that not only inspire but also challenge us to rethink the traditional paradigms of leadership. The stories featured in these pages are not just transforming their businesses and communities—they are redefining what leadership looks like in the modern world.

What resonates deeply with readers is the emphasis on the power of community and the collective impact we can achieve when we come together. As someone who has navigated the complexities of the corporate world, I've seen firsthand how critical it is for everyone to own the mission to deliver success. The stories shared are a powerful reminder that our greatest strength lies in our ability to connect, collaborate, and champion each other's wins.

"Grit and Tenacity" is not just a book -- it's a movement. It calls on each of us to embrace our full potential, lead with purpose, and make a lasting difference in the world around us. Cathy has given us a roadmap for how we can all contribute to a future where women are not only equal participants but leaders and trailblazers in every field.

I am honored to be part of this conversation and to witness the incredible impact that Cathy Derksen and the women in this book are making. May this book inspire everyone to lead with courage, compassion, and unwavering tenacity in delivering impact that matters.

Tricia Benn
Partner & Chief Executive Officer, C-Suite Network™, Podcast & TV Host, and Business Disruptor

Content

To small-town dreamers and silent survivors; To mentors illuminating paths; To women finding their voices:

Let this be a testament to the resilience of those rewriting their narratives, and may this story be a whisper of courage in your uncharted journey.

A Personal and Professional Journey Dedicated to Overcoming Circumstance

Michelle R. Zeiser Ph.D.

As I sit across from you, my old friend, in this cozy little coffee shop, I can't help but reflect on the journey that's brought me here. You know, coming from a small town in the Midwest, I was nestled in a cradle of conservative values and narrow perspectives. It was like living in a world sketched in black and white, unaware of the vibrant colors waiting out there. Growing up in rural Iowa, I was acutely aware of the traditional gender roles expected of me in the early 1990s – graduate high school, maybe go to college, get married, have kids, and become a homemaker, teacher, or nurse. However, I refused to be boxed in by societal expectations and focused on my education and career. Breaking free from this reality was no stroll in the park. It was more like climbing a mountain without a map. Education was my first rope. I delved into books and absorbed every bit of knowledge I could. My curiosity about things I didn't comprehend was my ticket to understanding a world beyond the rigid boundaries of my upbringing. How I showed up did not represent how I felt about myself. My feelings of uncontrollable shame began when an older male cousin began abusing me at age five. Ironically, at age five, it was the first time I was given alcohol by the hand of my abuser's mother at a family wedding. After that, I began comforting myself by eating uncontrollably and drinking at family functions like Thanksgiving, Christmas, and Easter, where I had to see my abuser. I can't remember if I told anyone about the abuse at that age, but I was thankful when the abuse stopped, but the shame still colors my trust in others to this day. My disordered eating and drinking offered an escape or compartmentalization from my pain, and it impeded my emotional growth.

Outwardly, I excelled in school, the national honor society, and extracurricular activities, but I was playing a role to fit in. My drinking became more disordered as a teen, and after high-school graduation, I lost my virginity to a boy who raped me in a blacked-out condition. In the 1990s, women were persecuted for drinking or how they dressed, and they brought it on themselves, versus men being held accountable for rape. I was publicly slut shamed but thankfully went off to college, intending never to return. When I got into a sorority, I got out, but my disordered eating and drinking escalated. When I dropped out of the sorority, I began working more than attending school and partied every night. The night I found out my grandmother died, I was caught underage at a bar I frequented with friends, and my shame spiraled deeper. I returned to my small-town home and started working a "real job" and carpooling with my mom until I could afford an apartment months later. While I failed to follow the traditional track of university after dropping out before my junior year, I embarked upon a decades-long thirst for education by taking night classes while rising through the ranks of multiple technology companies.

As you know, I have an innate ability to understand complex systems and was drawn to the world of computers and understanding people's motivations. So, when I dropped out of a traditional college at twenty-two, I lived up to the lowered expectations people had cast on me. My heart was broken from losing the grandmother who raised me. In school, I was working three service jobs to make ends meet, and my near-term goal was to make money, so I dropped out of school and started working in technology sales. I quickly discovered that I had a talent for sales and excelled in the fast-paced world of tech. I out-earned my parents' combined income and began pursuing my passions by studying psychology as an undergraduate in night school. While I quickly surpassed sales goals, became a manager, and united my interests in technology and human motivation, I failed to overcome the shame and feeling of not being enough that haunted my childhood.

By studying psychology as an undergraduate and earning two master's degrees in organizational leadership, development, and change, my intellectual curiosity created a window of insight. My focus was on strategy, technology, and innovation, and my education gave me the tools to challenge myself, expand my experience, and think critically.

Over the years, like you, I've had to navigate a male-dominated industry and work hard to prove myself. In my career coaching sales executives at high-tech companies, I often was the only woman in the room. There were times I was overlooked for promotions, not because I needed to gain skills but because I didn't fit into their mold of a traditional family-oriented woman. But I refused to let gender biases hold me back, and I worked to make a difference at multiple technology companies. My persistence has paid off; I have been elevated into senior leadership positions at each technology company, leading teams or strategy. Watching others ascend the career ladder, as their paths seemingly laid out for them, while I had to carve my own, was frustrating. But you know what? That made every success, every breakthrough sweeter. I learned to develop a growth mindset and to see each setback not as a failure but as a learning opportunity.

Mentorship and advocacy became a natural extension of my journey. I couldn't just climb the ladder and pull it up behind me. I had to reach down and help other women climb up, too. I started mentorship programs, gave talks on women's empowerment, and advocated for equitable practices in the workplace.

Traveling was the next leap. I moved from small-town Iowa to Denver, Colorado, and then to Seattle, Washington, seeking new experiences and finding myself. And remember when I first set foot on a new continent? It felt like I was stepping onto another planet. Every street, every face, every unfamiliar sound expanded my world lens, teaching me that diversity is not just to be tolerated but relished and celebrated. At thirty-six, I traveled solo to Italy, not knowing the language, and a decade before Google Translate or Maps. The beauty of global travel has offered me a peek into how others live and thrive in the world, reinforcing my belief that there is not just one right way to achieve or define success.

But it wasn't all smooth sailing, you know? Among the trials I faced was surviving an abusive marriage, a chapter of my life that remains shrouded in shadows, a narrative I rarely unfold. You see, living through physical, emotional, and sexual abuse is like being trapped in a relentless storm, where each day is a struggle to keep your head above water. The abuse shattered my confidence into a million pieces, leaving me to question my worth, my strength, and my very identity.

As challenging as it was, this period became a crucible that tested my strength in ways I never imagined. Every insult, every hurtful act, was like a hammer forging resilience in the core of my spirit. I learned the hard way that grit isn't just about enduring pain or surviving the day; it's about recognizing your own value and worth. It's about understanding that no amount of love or hope can fix someone who chooses to inflict pain.

Deciding to walk away was perhaps the bravest thing I've ever done. It wasn't just leaving a person; it was losing a home and financial burden that took me a decade to earn back. It was the moment I chose myself over the destructive cycle I was caught in. Walking away meant rediscovering my voice, reclaiming my power, and beginning the trying healing journey.

In that darkness, I found fragments of myself that I thought were lost forever. I pieced them back together, not as they were, but in a way that made me stronger, more compassionate, and more empathetic to myself and others. It was a slow and often painful process of rebuilding who I am from the ground up.

This experience, though I wouldn't wish it on anyone, taught me invaluable lessons about resilience. It taught me that true grit is about facing challenges head-on and having the courage to change your path when it leads to self-destruction. It's about knowing when to fight and when to take flight for the sake of your own well-being. And in that flight, I found my wings, wings that have since carried me to heights I never imagined possible.

My story is a testament to the power of hard work, perseverance, and a refusal to be limited by one's circumstances. I defied the statistics, built a successful career in the tech industry, and continue to inspire countless others to follow in my footsteps.

Despite my resilience, my life experiences created a skewed trust towards people in perceived power. I have learned to balance my bias using therapeutic techniques such as meditation, therapy, exercise, and yoga. I recognize how self-medication with disordered eating, alcohol, and avoidance limited my progression, and I work hard every day to overcome these challenges.

My professional, educational, and life experiences have taught me to celebrate all the experiences that make me unique and one of a kind. I embrace a growth mindset when I experience setbacks and failure, utilizing critical discovery techniques to understand and move forward. I know now that resilience comes from within and requires continuous self-reflection, growth, and learning.

My journey is just one of many women who survived abuse and demonstrates the power of perseverance and the importance of developing resilience in the face of adversity. Despite my challenging background, I've built a meaningful career and remained determined to learn and grow personally - proving that anyone can overcome obstacles and achieve their goals with grit and tenacity.

Reflecting on my journey, it's astonishing to realize that well over 550 days ago, I reached a monumental milestone in my life – achieving sobriety. This achievement wasn't just about putting an end to a habit; it was about reclaiming control over my life, about breaking free from the chains that had held me captive for far too long.

Sobriety, for me, was like emerging from a haze. Each sober day was a step towards clarity, towards understanding myself and the world around me without the distorted lens of substance abuse. It was a journey of rediscovering joys and pleasures in their purest form, unmarred by artificial stimulants and the cycle of anxiety and depression it brings.

But my battle wasn't just with substance abuse. Alongside it, I also wrestled with disordered eating. This was another demon that lurked in the shadows, skewing my relationship with food and body image. Overcoming this was like navigating a labyrinth filled with societal pressures, personal insecurities, and a constant internal battle between self-care and self-destruction.

Managing my disordered eating meant learning to treat food not as an enemy or a coping mechanism but as a source of nourishment and fuel. It involved unlearning toxic patterns and rebuilding a healthier, more compassionate relationship with my body and mind. It was about tuning in to my body's needs, respecting its signals, and honoring it for its looks and its incredible functions.

The combined challenge of maintaining sobriety and managing disordered eating was a journey of holistic healing. It wasn't just about abstaining or regulating; it was about transforming my entire lifestyle, my thought processes, and my coping mechanisms. It required building a support system, seeking professional help, and, most importantly, cultivating a relentless commitment to self-care and self-love.

Looking back over this time, I see a path marked with struggles but, more importantly, victories. Each day has been a testament to my resilience and dedication to a healthier, happier life. This journey has taught me about the strength of the human spirit and the power of determination. It has shown me that healing is possible, change is attainable, and a better life is within reach. As I continue this path, I carry the lessons learned, the strength gained, and the grace every new day brings.

As you know, exercise has been a constant in my life, and since my hip replacement in my early 40s, I've transformed my approach to self-care. I can't help but marvel at the pivotal role my Peloton bike, walking, yoga, and meditation have played in my journey. These activities have been a cornerstone in rebuilding and nurturing my physical and mental well-being.

The Peloton bike was a game changer. It became more than just a piece of exercise equipment; it was a vehicle of transformation. The empowering instructors, the diverse community, and the convenience of hopping on the bike anytime made fitness accessible and enjoyable. It was no longer about punishing my body but celebrating its capabilities. Each session on the Peloton was a step towards better health and a moment to disconnect from the stressors of daily life.

Walking, in its simplicity, was equally transformative. It became my time for reflection, spending time with my pups, and connection with nature. Whether it was a brisk walk in the morning or a quick stroll in the evening, each step was a chance to breathe in fresh air, clear my mind, and appreciate the world around me. Walking has turned into a meditative practice, a way to center myself and find peace in the rhythm of my footsteps or time to catch up on podcasts.

Yoga, on the other hand, has been a lifelong journey of harmony between mind and body. It helped me survive my divorce and has centered me through each life-changing event throughout my journey. It has taught me to embrace flexibility, not just physically but in every aspect of life. Through various poses and breathing techniques, yoga has allowed me to explore my body's limits, stretch and strengthen, and find balance. It continues to be a sanctuary where I can nurture inner calm and resilience, learning to flow with life's ups and downs.

Meditation is the most profound of all my self-care practices. Sitting still began as a challenge, trying to quiet the mind's endless chatter. But with time, it has evolved into a profound experience of self-awareness and mindfulness. Meditation has given me the tools to observe my thoughts without judgment, to find stillness amidst chaos, and to cultivate a sense of inner peace. It is a daily ritual, from deep breaths to center to a few moments dedicated entirely to my mental and emotional well-being.

These practices, whether riding, walking, yoga, or meditation, have transformed my approach to self-care. They taught me that caring for myself is not just a physical act but an emotional and spiritual one. They have been vital in managing stress, improving my mood, and boosting my overall health. More importantly, they taught me the value of taking time for myself, listening to my body and mind, and the incredible strength and peace in self-care routines.

It's funny, in a way, how life comes full circle. I left my small town to explore the vast world, only to realize that my mission was to make that world a little more accessible and a little more equitable for those who come after me. So here I am, decades into this journey, still learning, still growing. And if there's one thing I could pass on, it's this: never underestimate the power of a woman determined to rise. Because, my friend, we're not just breaking free from the molds; we're reshaping them for generations to come.

Author Bio

Michelle R. Zeiser Ph.D.

Michelle R. Zeiser Ph.D. is a respected scholar-practitioner known for her expertise in addressing gender disparity in the workplace, with a particular focus on growth mindset, resilience, and change leadership. Hailing from a small town in the Midwest, Zeiser's childhood was characterized by an insatiable love for reading and a strong passion for learning, which she nurtured through extensive education, travel, and leadership coaching at technology companies.

Her academic journey led to a vital dissertation examining how leaders who self-identify as women adapt and build resilience amidst technological changes and workplace transitions. This work established Zeiser as a leading voice, skilled researcher, and storyteller adept at unraveling the complexities of human experience and the process of sensemaking in complex environments.

Beyond her academic accomplishments, Zeiser is a passionate advocate for women in technology. She is actively involved on boards, leading workshops and seminars, mentoring and empowering women in tech to pursue their ambitions and amplify their voices.

Zeiser's multifaceted career and contributions highlight her as a visionary in both scholarly realms and social advocacy, with her work profoundly influencing the discourse around gender dynamics in professional settings and women's empowerment at technology companies and the future of work.

- linkedin.com/in/michellezeiser/

I dedicate this book to sponsors who have opened doors for me and offered me seats at the table when I would have not had them otherwise. I honor you commitment to a gender equitable future by paying it forward.

Sponsorship is Not a Buzzword; It's A Verb

Victoria Vojnovich

I was raised to believe that "to whom much is given, much is expected." It is something I think about daily and try to live up to. Now, don't get me wrong, it has taken a lot of work to get to where I am today. I am a first-generation American, the first in my family to attend university, and I financed my education entirely on my own. I got a degree in STEM at a time when women's representation in STEM degree programs was quite small, even at large public universities. Despite these challenges, I have been incredibly fortunate to have a successful career, a good marriage, three amazing children who are my greatest accomplishments, and plenty of blessings along the way.

Of course, I have had my share of setbacks and heartache. After years of infertility, I was thrilled to finally have a sustainable pregnancy in progress when my oldest daughter decided that a 40-week pregnancy was not in her plan and showed up at 23 weeks. Her 134-day NICU stay was a rollercoaster of stress, near-death moments, astonishing recoveries, and some lifelong challenges, including deafness, reactive airway disease, a mild seizure disorder, and the autism spectrum. And yet, she has a bachelor's degree, is pursuing a second one, is breaking ground in the area of access and equity in the arts and is a joy to all who know her.

Three years later, her brother decided to show up even a week earlier. Unfortunately, he was simply too premature, and he died about 2.5 hours after his birth. I feel his spirit with me every day. A surprise twin pregnancy one year later resulted in 15 weeks of total bed rest and a set of 29-week preemie twins, who were miraculously healthy despite a 57-day NICU stay. However, they also have a preemie tax; both have severe ADHD and anxiety. They are amazing humans, successful and kind, leaders in their own right.

For the sake of my family and because I had worked so hard to be a mom, I took a leave from the paid workforce to concentrate on giving these special humans a great start in their lives. After all, they worked really hard to stay here; it was the right thing to do. I will never regret this decision. What I was most surprised to discover was that when my children were settled into preschool and elementary school were on their way, and I had decided to return to the paid workforce, the roadblocks that I faced were insurmountable. Frankly, I was beyond surprised; I was shocked and highly disappointed.

Before taking my leave, I was quite successful in my career. I was deemed by my company "an executive resource," which gave me access to executive mentoring, rotational programs, additional training and development, and opportunities for positions with the corporate staff (opportunities usually reserved for employees significantly more experienced and advanced in their careers).

I was well-liked, received outstanding performance appraisals, and was sought after for my reputation as a person who could turn challenges into successes. After I took my career break, I was viewed as obsolete, not committed to my career, and no longer executive material. This was despite my getting additional certifications while I was on leave, starting my own consulting company, and securing contracts from some large companies for consulting services.

So what did I do? How did I recover and get to where I am today? First, I took a deep breath. I had a company and was doing some consulting, and it was going well. While I had hoped to return to the corporate world, a place where I was comfortable and felt that I could make the most difference, I realized that I needed to show more people what I could do. So I started investing full-time in my company. I joined a networking organization. I created some case studies featuring my clients and got some speaking engagements at international conferences. That was my breakthrough.

While at an International Coach Federation conference, where I was presenting at a breakout, I met a corporate leader who was looking to build an internal coaching program and asked me to meet her for dinner. We discussed my corporate experience and how I could parlay my consulting and corporate experience into a new strategic initiative in her company. Three weeks later, I had an offer and started with that company.

As I pondered that encounter and the resultant offer, I uncovered the one key reason that I received this offer: the person who hired me was a woman. In our dinner conversation, after she talked to me about the opportunity, I decided to be very transparent about my criteria to accept the offer. I had three high-needs children. Yes, they were all in preschool or elementary school. Yes, I had after-school care, who picked them up from school, took them to their activities, helped my oldest with homework, and even started dinner. AND, they had medical appointments (many medical appointments for my oldest), therapy appointments, early intervention appointments, IEP meetings, and a pile of other things. I was not willing to buck these out to others. Flexibility had to be an option. I would gladly travel for business, hold meetings early in the morning and late at night, and give 150% of my energy and passion. I would be respectful and notify my colleagues when I had to attend an appointment for my kids. However, it had to be understood that emergencies would likely arise and that I needed to have the flexibility to manage those emergencies.

Had this initial meeting been held by a man, I am positive that my commitment to the company and the job would have been questioned, the person would have paid for a nice dinner, we would have shaken hands, and I would not have received the offer. Instead, my hiring manager, also a mother of young children, understood the assignment. She hired me on the value that I would bring to the job and committed to sponsoring me and my work with the flexibility I needed to be successful. For my part in this relationship, I delivered superior results, grew the program, and led our team to global recognition. It was a win-win. She got promoted, I got promoted, and both of us received tons of recognition and opportunity. And it was the start of my career-long commitment to sponsorship, both receiving and offering sponsorship.

And yet, 20-plus years later, it is still remarkably difficult for women who take a career break to re-enter the paid workforce, and sponsorship of women in the workplace is still nowhere near where it needs to be. Only 10 percent of the Fortune 500 companies offer a formal re-entry program, and even when they do, the programs bring women returners in essentially as new hires. The companies benefit from their experience and maturity, but salaries and benefits are not reflective of that experience. While women are away from the workforce, they are not building their Social Security or any other social safety net, and restarting their careers at low salary points puts them at risk at retirement age.

Formal sponsorship is even more rare. While many companies finally realize the value of employee resource groups, many ERGs are still seen as social networks rather than business-building organizations, where skills, leadership capabilities, and future leaders can be nurtured and developed. Sometimes, informal sponsorship relationships come from these networks. However, in some industries, such as tech, women's participation in the field continues to stagnate at ~25%, and women in leadership in this field continue to stagnate at ~10%.

The COVID-19 pandemic has further impacted women in the workforce, as women left the paid workforce at a ~35% higher rate than men due to job stress combined with increased responsibilities at home. Many of these women want to return to the paid workforce but are being hired back at new-hire salaries.

The United Nations determined that global gender equality was set back almost 50 years as a result of the pandemic. McKinsey and Company's annual "Women in the Workplace" reports for 2021 - 2023 have noted two critical trends: 1) women still have a solid barrier to leadership entry at the first-line manager role, and 2) women at the director and above levels are still leaving their roles at high levels due to inflexibility on behalf of the companies they work for. In both reports, McKinsey recommends hybrid working and other flexibility programs as well as formal sponsorship programs as ways to close both these gaps.

I am grateful for every woman leader who has sponsored me in my career, and I make a point to mention them by name on LinkedIn every International Women's Day. Some of my Ph.D. research is on returnship programs for women, where we can take a deeper look at crediting women for the experience they bring back to a company in terms of salary and benefits upon rehire while also formalizing through policy and incentives structured re-entry programs as a normal way of running a business. This research has contributed to my dissertation study, "Reimagining the Future of Work for Mid-to-Late Career Women."

And I actively sponsor women at my company. Sponsorship is a verb. It's not mentoring (skills building); it's representation. It's making sure that the person you are sponsoring is considered for opportunities when they are not in the room. It is providing opportunities for visibility, stretch assignments, and recognition in all those spaces that might otherwise be closed. It's offering a seat at the table when they would typically be on the periphery of the room if they are even in the room in the first place. If every woman leader made a commitment to sponsor at least one other woman, our impact would be exponential. I challenge you to join me in a sponsorship challenge. Choose one woman in your business or community who does not have a seat or a voice at the table and offer it on their behalf. Let's bring about equity for women, one sponsorship at a time!

Author Bio

Victoria Vojnovich

Victoria Vojnovich is the founder and CEO of iEmpowHer, LLC. She is committed to bridging the global gender equality gap for women in the workforce and re-imagining the future of work to create equitable workspaces for all. Having spent her entire career in Tech, Victoria understands the value of mentorship and sponsorship for women, who still only make up 23% of the tech workforce (and unfortunately, only 10% of leadership roles in tech). In the five companies where she has worked, she has led or sponsored the women's employee resource groups to support women's' professional growth and development in a safe and nurturing space.

Victoria also leads a global cloud services transformation office for an Indian headquartered global systems integrator (GSI). She holds a Professional Certified Coach (PCC) designation from the International Coach Federation, among multiple certifications and designations. She is also a member of Chief, the largest network of senior women executives. Vojnovich has a B.S. degree in Mathematics and Computer Science from Penn State University, an M.A. degree in Women's and Gender Studies from North Carolina State University and is completing her PhD program at North Carolina State University, where her dissertation research topic is "Re-Imagining the Future of Work for Mid-to-Late Career Women".

Victoria lives in Cary, NC with her husband, and her three adult children live nearby. She is an avid football fan and can be found cheering on her Penn State Nittany Lions and Philadelphia Eagles every weekend throughout the fall and winter.

- iempowher.net
- linkedin.com/in/victoriavojnovich

I dedicate this chapter to all the world's youth those alive, and ones yet to be born - especially Katherine and Michael. To people who imagine our world working for all and live their lives as if it is true.

Shifting Inequitable Systems Through Community Engagement

Karin Tice, Ph.D.

"Never doubt that a small group of thoughtful, committed citizens [people] can change the world. Indeed, it's the only thing that ever has."

- Margaret Mead, used with permission

"Change the story, change the world."

- Karin Tice

Introduction

Women leaders in philanthropy, the nonprofit sector, and those working at the grassroots level in their neighborhoods, communities[1], cities, and businesses have an unprecedented opportunity to create a world that works for everyone. To reweave the global social fabric into a multicultural tapestry where everyone can thrive and contribute their unique gifts.

As the world falls apart, women are rising. They are creating highly innovative solutions in healthcare, climate change, food systems, education, housing, STEM, and almost every other issue area. Our work is urgent, and our success is critical to the world's future. We do not have the luxury of investing in incremental change.

Transformational leaders desiring to create equitable systems need to know the extent to which their work is making a difference. What strategies are working well? What is not working? What needs to

---

1   I am using "community" in a colloquial way to refer to towns and cities. Community is a complex, highly nuanced term. I will explore these complexities in a future publication.

be strengthened or completely changed? Are we making a difference? What are the next actionable steps to help us move forward?

Creating a world that works for everyone requires us to work in creative and imaginative ways across silos and cultures to innovate and learn together. We need to work in an inclusive and equitable manner so that each leader can bring her best to the table. Co-created solutions can be transformational. "If you want to go fast, go alone; if you want to go far, go together." (An African proverb)

I hope my story inspires you to take action and reach out to other women to work in new ways across silos and differences. This chapter will: 1) tell you about Formative Evaluation Research Associates (FERA's) approach to catalyzing systems change for a just and equitable world that works for everyone; 2) share my own leadership journey; 3) offer words of wisdom related to working together across silos; and 4) end with a call to action.

About FERA

Formative Evaluation Research Associates (FERA) is a creative, nimble business that began 50 years ago with a social justice focus and the audacious goal of touching every major social issue of our time. We support pilot efforts to be strong and effective before they are scaled, recognizing that whenever you try a new solution, it seldom works the way initially envisioned. Developmental evaluation is ongoing and supports innovation and adaptation in dynamic environments. FERA shares effective practices with enough context so that other innovators can consider relevance to their work. Our approach contributes to expanded partnerships, and increased investment of resources as existing and potential funders and partners understand the value of an initiative and why it matters—deeper and more far-reaching outcomes.

FERA does evaluation and learning with people, not to them. We move at the speed of trust and honor local knowledge and expertise. We engage people across differences to interpret the data we collect and develop actionable recommendations. We weave and share inspirational, hopeful stories of towns and cities that are shifting their narratives and stepping into new stories about what is possible.

FERA began in 1973 when, mirroring our current world, unrest, and turmoil had been tearing apart our social fabric. Police brutality, inequitable living conditions, and unjust systems lead to the racial uprisings in the 1960s, Vietnam War protests, and the women's movement. Within this context, FERA asked - How can we use evaluation to make the world a better place for everyone? How can we make the data we collect useful to changemakers (local leaders, nonprofits, intermediaries, foundations, and their partners)? How can evaluation serve as a catalyst for change?

Funders often require external independent evaluation. When FERA started, evaluations typically occurred at the end of a program, producing lengthy reports full of statistics that collected dust on a shelf or were stuffed into a drawer—completed but never used. Although the field of evaluation has been shifting, those engaged in highly innovative work still often feel "done to" by evaluators and other consultants who have positioned themselves as "experts" and do not value local knowledge and experiences.

FERA's clients are trying to solve complex problems in new ways. Social innovators and their supporters want to know which group's strategies are effective and explore ways to strengthen or adjust efforts in real time. Pilot initiatives need to be as effective as possible before being scaled. Questions we often answer include—To what extent are we making a difference, and for whom? Are outcomes different by race/ethnicity, gender, geographic location, or other factors? What are the root causes underlying this issue? Why does this work matter?

FERA works with organizations, systems, cities, and states at the local, national, and international levels. We support initiatives designed to address inequities by creating new opportunities as well as advocating for policy changes in multiple areas including education, STEM, healthcare, workforce development, and philanthropic and nonprofit infrastructure. We bring our expertise in evaluation and learning to the table while the people we engage are the experts in their fields. When we partner, we create robust learning opportunities. We can tell a powerful story that can be used to access funding, expand partnerships, and share with others attempting similar work in other places.

FERA's approach is participatory and designed to be useful. We engage stakeholders (e.g., staff, board members, community partners, participants, and funders) in a process to shape the evaluation's scope and focus. A facilitated data interpretation workshop re-engages stakeholders to make meaning of the data collected and develop actionable recommendations. FERA developed these two processes 50+ years ago. We find that our approach increases buy-in, brings people together often across differences, and can catalyze positive change.

We recognize the importance of diverse perspectives and experiences in shaping understanding and creating useful recommendations.

My Story

As a woman business leader, I believe it is not only possible but essential to catalyze change that moves us towards an equitable, socially just, and sustainable world. I'm an applied social anthropologist, and no, I don't dig up bones. Weaving stories about transformative and inspirational efforts led often by small groups of people who have visions for a world where all people can thrive is my passion.

Over the years, I lost my voice, became invisible, and felt like I belonged nowhere. By re-interpreting my story's meaning, I realized that I belong everywhere because I'm curious and love connecting with people from different cultures. I often serve as a bridge and a translator across cultures and other ways people are diverse. I've found my voice and gained the courage to step into visibility by showing up with a full heart, risking being vulnerable, knowing my own worth, and sharing my ideas as I'm doing in this chapter. As I show up differently, abundance of all types increasingly flows into my life. I run my business with passion and purpose at the center. I believe in pursuing the triple bottom line of people, planet, and prosperity.

I lead and own Formative Evaluation Research Associates (FERA), a nearly seven-figure business that supports innovative systems change efforts. I consider myself a social entrepreneur. I am at the heart of the business; we grew together.

You might wonder how I, an applied social anthropologist, became President and Owner of FERA. One day, I took a break from writing my book Kuna Crafts, Gender and the Global Economy—exploring the dynamic intersection of gender, class, ethnicity, and globalization. The Kuna (now spelled Guna) are an indigenous group living in an archipelago of tiny islands and mainland jungle off the coast of Panama. I went to a gathering where a friend who worked for FERA asked me if I could conduct interviews on a part-time basis; they needed extra help. I said yes! FERA hired me as a research assistant. Within a month, I became full-time. That happened over four decades ago, and now I own the company.

I never wanted to own or run a business, but my FERA business partner wanted to retire and couldn't find a buyer. I knew if I wanted to continue doing the work I loved and felt passionate about, I would have to step into leadership, buy out my partner, and lead the firm. I had no business background and never considered myself to be part of the business world. I didn't know at the time that I had both leadership and entrepreneurial skills and qualities.

I purchased FERA in 2007 and developed a strategic vision with the intention of focusing on a few select issues I cared about. I felt excited and ready to move forward when the economic crash of 2008 hit. No one, not even seasoned professionals with more experience than I, received contracts. I knew I had to do something dramatically different. First, I tossed my beautifully crafted plan into a bottom drawer. Then, I accepted any project that came my way, big or small, any topic.

Leadership Obstacles/Challenges

Entrepreneurial skills are not my greatest challenge... I lead a highly successful triple-bottom-line business. My biggest struggles are internal.

- I didn't see myself as an entrepreneur or businesswoman. I work with nonprofits, philanthropists, and their community partners, and while business needs to be at the table to solve social issues, they are often not present. I ran FERA like a nonprofit. Until recently, I didn't interact with the business community or access resources and networks to support FERA's growth. Leading FERA outside of standard models allowed me to create a woman-centered business and approach to my work. For example, when I was pregnant 30 years ago and put on bed rest, FERA experimented and then shifted to a virtual business model. This way of working also benefits other FERA consultants who want to combine work they are passionate about with caring for children and elders.

- I was invisible, and so was FERA. Until recently, I have not widely shared FERA's approaches and why they matter. As I reclaim my voice, I'm stepping into visibility in new ways. I'm learning to clearly communicate how FERA adds value. I'm willing to speak out even when I don't know how my words will be received (writing this chapter, for example).

- What I know now is that my self-worth is determined internally, not externally. When I do not succeed, I've learned to use the same curious, learning mindset I use with the initiatives I support, asking myself - I wonder what went wrong? I wonder what I could do differently or what I need to learn or practice for next time? Is this my work to do?

- FERA and I both work outside of the box. For decades, foundations valued big data. I have spent my entire career sharing qualitative stories interwoven with quantitative data, highlighting the root causes of a problem and expected and unexpected outcomes, providing enough context so that others can consider how a similar initiative might work elsewhere, and sharing lessons learned. These stories help the reader understand the value and importance of the work...why it matters. It wasn't easy to stay true to what I knew created the most value. I'm still working on the best way to tell my/FERA's story. I now realize my differences are my greatest assets.

- Social context. I want to acknowledge that as a woman in a white body with access to many resources and opportunities, I've had privileges that black and brown women often do not have. At the same time, as a woman, I have encountered social stereotypes. I was discouraged from pursuing a Ph.D. and told that being a secretary might be a better fit for me. While I highly value an effective assistant, those are not the skills I bring to the world. I've been told my bids were "too expensive," while male colleagues with less experience and fewer credentials who charged more were considered "highly professional" and worth the cost. Women, myself included, are typically raised to put our needs last, if at all. Advocating for myself and the value I bring has been a growth edge for me. It has required me to create new internal stories.

Words of Wisdom

You might be wondering, what can I do? Here is what worked for me.

- Let your values and passion for making the world a better place for everyone drive your business decisions. Be generous and, at the same time, ask for what you're worth. Get clear about and share the value you bring. If you add exceptional value ... money flows.

- I believe that social change happens when people gather around the "kitchen table" to take actions, however big or small.

- Listen deeply and co-create—focus on strengths and assets while acknowledging the history that created inequities along the lines of race, gender, and class.

- Creativity and working outside the box are critically important skills for innovation and entrepreneurship.

- Consider what are your most extraordinary qualities and life experiences. Ask others – it can be hard to see yourself.

- Walk your talk...We work with initiatives designed to support families and children. FERA is a family-friendly place to work. We support small local businesses whenever possible.

- You don't need to know everything. Reach out and ask for resources and support. Create or join networks that can serve this purpose.

- Relationships matter. Engage with people. Don't assume you know anything. Ask. Be culturally responsive in your business practices. Find opportunities to engage in racial healing work. Show up authentically with an open heart, willing to listen, to see people deeply, to be curious, and to turn to wonder.

- Understand the nuances of the "communities" you serve...where are the internal "borders"? What are the old stories about who does or does not belong? What are new stories about what is possible?

- Be bold! Be willing to transform your old stories about what is possible in your own business and life.

- Stories are powerful.... imagine new stories—change the story, change the world.

Call to Action

What if women leaders in communities and businesses worked together to create spaces where everyone felt welcomed and like they had a place at the table? What if we sat at each other's kitchen tables to co-create solutions to global issues, learn and support each other, and create new friendships by reaching out across differences and finding what we share? These new relationships can catalyze a just and sustainable world while simultaneously enriching and bringing joy into our own lives. What if we created public spaces where everyone felt a sense of belonging and possibility?

We all have threads that can be used to reweave our global social fabric into a magnificent new multi-colored tapestry ...What are yours?

Author Bio

Karin Tice, Ph.D.

Dr. Karin Tice, Ph.D., is a thought leader and social artist who uses evaluation & learning to catalyze a socially just world that works for everyone. Karin leads and owns Formative Evaluation Research Associates (FERA) www.feraonline.com. FERA is 100% woman-owned and is celebrating 50+ years partnering with leaders, nonprofits, and foundations. FERA engages with diverse communities, building bridges and weaving stories of hope that inspire action.

Karin has a Ph.D. in Applied Social Anthropology and Education from Columbia University/Teachers College. Her book, Kuna Crafts, Gender, and the Global Economy, published by the University of Texas Press, Austin, TX., received the American Library Association Award for best academic book of the year (1995). Karin's evaluation research has been published, disseminated, and used to inform systems change worldwide.

Karin has lived or conducted research in Mexico, the Mayan highlands of Guatemala, Guna Yala (previously Kuna Yala), an autonomous indigenous territory in Panama, Cataluña, Spain, and Switzerland for a total of 11 years over her lifetime. She is bilingual in Spanish and English and has a working knowledge of Catalan, Italian, and two indigenous languages spoken in Guatemala and Panama. As a result, she has experienced different ways of knowing, being, and learning. She is a creative leader who leads from her heart, thinks outside the box, and works cross-culturally.

- linkedin.com/in/karin-tice-1bb7218/

Dedicated to my sweet girls, Norah and Stella.

To my Mom, Dad, and Brenda for always being there.

Grateful for my family and friends for supporting the

'DIVA' in me.

Igniting Your Inner DIVA

Nicole Scheffler

In a world where challenges and opportunities dance together in our daily lives, it's important to remember that you control your destiny. As the Tech Diva, my career path has been paved by grit, illuminated by tenacity, and enriched by my unique experiences. Like many of you, I enjoyed my formal education, obtaining undergraduate and master's degrees in the technology field where I was always fascinated by how things work as a system and how we can create a better future. I had all the tangible skills to find success in my career, but things changed when I looked within and brought my whole self into all aspects of my life, showing up authentically everywhere.

I simply felt more fulfilled when I recognized and harnessed my innate gifts and qualities like empathy, intuition, and collaboration. This approach has been pivotal to my overcoming my own obstacles, evolving personally, and ultimately finding more success. It was one thing to have achievements, but it is so much better now that I am in alignment with who I am and the impact I make on the world.

What is your gift?

My personal life mission is to ignite success for women by being a leader in the field of cyber security and by serving others through the Tech Diva Success inspirational collection. A deep appreciation for life's blessings and an openness to learn and grow have helped me pursue success on my terms. I offer you insights into my leadership journey and the lessons I learned along the way. My wish is for you to uncover your inherent gifts, enabling you to radiate your Light both professionally and personally.

The Web I Weaved

As a 1980s baby, technology was a significant influence in my life. During my formative years, rapidly evolving technology fascinated me and is still at the center of my career. I grew up during the dawn of the Internet. To play a game on a computer, I would follow a series of prompts from a sticky note on the monitor. I used cheat codes (some even required game genie hardware) and remember playing with ELIZA, the first iteration of a chatbot. Back then, my friends and I had a good laugh at early AI. We did not have Google or YouTube videos to help us through life, so I learned to problem-solve for the future by simply creating it.

I fell in love with technology and worked in networking, which consisted of hardware (like routers) and software (like an Operating System). I realized that hardware and software provide a great analogy for life. Our bodies are simply the hardware we are given and require maintenance – like diet or fitness – to keep them working in optimum form. They work just like any hardware in that they age, need upgrades, and benefit from innovations. Our minds are the software working with our bodies to help us function. Our software constantly needs small tweaks and upgrades from continuous learning, working with counselors, doing personal development, and incorporating our life experiences.

If you want to get super nerdy, I will say there's an additional cybersecurity analogy here. When negative things like viruses and mental illness compromise our bodies or minds, we must identify and stop those intrusive thoughts or infections right away to thrive. In all cases, we are the only ones responsible for maintaining our hardware and software in life to ensure we get the most longevity from our physical and mental biology.

With my college degree and the opportunities that followed, I discovered myself living the "American dream" narrative. After I obtained my master's degree, I landed a job at Cisco Systems as a Systems Engineer building world-class network architectures for major global companies. I am grateful for this chapter, and I still have the keychain my mom gave me that had "engineer" engraved in a single silver heart. Her pride in me fuels me even today, and the experience I gained in the associate program was priceless.

At this point in my early career, I realized nothing was stopping me from being a leader in my community and gaining critical skills by volunteering for causes I cared about. I decided to use community service as a training tool for leadership in philanthropy and business. Happy volunteers indicate good leadership, and this work brought me great joy.

About a decade into my career, I found myself contributing to those same programs as a leader. I started two community technology groups and one full non-profit. This instilled in me a mindset of servant leadership that I feel is embedded in my operating system.

I continued proudly working as an individual contributor, believing every good team needed passionate, dependable players, and I enjoyed the game. However, it was time to move from being a solid team player to creating the team. At this point in my career, someone thankfully took a chance on me and offered me my first manager position. I was given an opportunity to serve in a strategy and planning role while nurturing a highly skilled engineering team.

I was lucky to work with many leaders throughout my career. I learned the power of humility and the impact you make by stopping to recognize moments that matter for your team, which could be in work or in life. Not only did I learn so much working with senior leadership, but I also knew I wanted to embed this intentionality into my leadership practices.

Just as software faces failures and needs upgrades, my programming was tested during the 2020 pandemic. Leading up to the birth of my second child that fall, life threw me numerous curveballs that tested my resilience, as it did for many of you. I grappled with the isolation of remote life, the responsibilities of caring for my firstborn while working from home, and the fears stemming from my severe asthma. In addition, my father received a cancer diagnosis, and my stepmother was in a coma in the ICU for months with COVID-19. Tragically, less than a week before welcoming our new baby, my mother-in-law passed away from cancer. As it goes, some of the biggest challenges in life, our tower moments, are there to pave the way for greatness.

Amidst this tumultuous period, my new precious baby reminded me about the beauty of life. I am so grateful for her Light during one of my darkest periods. Only weeks after welcoming her to this world, I received the jarring news that my job had decided to eliminate my role immediately upon my return from maternity leave. As the primary breadwinner for my family, I was now faced with uncertainty and the huge responsibility of securing a means of supporting my loved ones at the height of a global pandemic.

As a woman and an ally for all women, this series of events was a blow to my spirit. It was a stark reminder of the challenges women continue to face in the workplace, particularly during pivotal life moments like motherhood. However, I was determined to turn adversity into opportunity. It was time to apply the grit and tenacity that had brought me this far. That is when the Tech Diva was truly born, and another upgrade was in progress for my operating system.

I found two keys to success during this hard time: having support systems and the power of mindset. Support came in the form of good friends, Zoom communities, and even remote baby showers. It was during this time that I became committed to always helping others in the same way I had been supported. It's amazing what a short text, phone call, or a simple Snapchat can do to change your day for the better.

My mindset is what changed the most. In the lonely months of weird isolation early in the pandemic, I found myself walking a lot outside and listening to motivational books like *Think and Grow Rich* by Napoleon Hill and *The Success Principles* by Jack Canfield. I truly wanted to start manifesting the life of my dreams. These words of wisdom awakened my power to own who I am in life with intention and vision. I didn't just create the Tech Diva; I became her.

I created a plan, stayed relentless in my pursuit of success, and elevated my advocacy for women in tech. During this 'upgrade' period, I earned my Success Coach certification and published my first book with my mentor, Jack Canfield. I am proof that even in the face of immense adversity, we can harness our inner grit to survive, thrive, and empower others along the way. I chose to upgrade my software by listening and embodying the success principles I was studying, like the laws of attraction and visioning. Maintaining our operating systems is a continuous task that never truly ends.

My Lessons Learned

I want to share a simple formula you can master to turn any event in your life into an opportunity to learn and grow. This formula could even hold the keys to a happier life: E + R = O.

Events + Responses = Outcomes

Events happen to us every day, with challenges and opportunities presenting themselves at every moment. We decide how to respond to these events, and we can choose to keep small issues insignificant or blow them out of proportion. Our response is our true point of power. The outcome can be influenced simply by how we react.

How can you make the outcome in your favor? Remember, you are in control.

Adversity is inevitable, but how we respond makes the difference. Most people will blame, complain, or make excuses to avoid accountability, but these responses don't serve any purpose in the big picture.

If you start to look at every interaction in your day and evaluate your reactions and the corresponding outcomes, you can assess the behavior patterns and adjust your responses accordingly. This allows you to live a happier and fulfilled life.

Another secret to success is to level up your goal-setting with visualizations. Visualization is the act of envisioning yourself achieving your biggest goals as you work to accomplish them.

How can you create a life you love if you don't know what that life is?

I encourage you to spend a few minutes, close your eyes, and imagine a day of living the life of your dreams. Play out your entire day from when you wake up until you go to sleep at night, feeling and seeing it as if you were really there.

- What do you see when you open your eyes?

- Who is by your side?

- What are the details you see in your home or work environment?

- What activities do you do throughout the day?

- Who do you work with?

- How do you spend your free time?

- What brings you joy?

Everything you envision and all the attached feelings are the first step to building an amazing life by design. You should set your goals, have a clear vision, and then take small steps daily toward that vision until it becomes your reality. It is important to go beyond just imagining what you want; it is also important to know how it makes you feel once you have it.

You are responsible for maintaining your hardware and software, so get to know and love it since that is all you have. I realize that you don't turn a switch and become tenacious. You must take care of yourself by prioritizing self-care. As we all know too well, you cannot pour from an empty cup. You have no choice but to show up for yourself, your life, and your loved ones every day. The attitude you approach life with makes all the difference.

I saved the biggest lesson for last. Life starts and ends with you. It's easy to spread love and want to help others—our children, coworkers, etc. It is much harder to simply love yourself. We tend to let our fire go out when we are facing judgment or dealing with hard things. The most important lesson for a Diva's success is fully loving yourself for all your amazing gifts. It's these gifts that will help shape the future of technology and our world. It's time for all Divas to rise!

WOMANifesto: Igniting the DIVA Within

The time is NOW to ignite your DIVA within and let your fire burn bright. For in its glow lies the power to inspire, innovate, and lead the way toward a future where every woman's flame shines fiercely.

Divine

You are divine.

In the flicker of your soul lies the divine spark, the ember waiting to ignite. What sets you ablaze? What fuels your passion and lights up your being? Your inherent gifts, those precious kindlings bestowed upon you, are the very essence of your fire. Your presence, a gift of life, radiates with the potential to illuminate the world. Live it, nurture it, and tend to it diligently, for within you lies the power to make change greater than you can imagine. Women carry a special warmth that can nurture and connect us to a better future.

Inspired

Be inspired.

In the dance of flames, we find ourselves mesmerized with inspiration. We are inspired by the women who came before us; their stories etched into the fabric of time: each fire, a testament to their resilience, their strength. But inspiration isn't confined to the past; it thrives in the present and blooms in the future. Every young girl is a reason to ignite our fire and pave the way for a brighter tomorrow. Together, we shine bright, fanning each other's flames, creating a collective vision of possibility. Once you find your spark, use it to fill your heart and carry your gifts into the world.

Vision

Seek your vision.

In the glow of your fire, envision the path ahead. Feel it coursing through your veins, guiding your steps with purpose and intention. Define success on your terms, not by society's standards, but by the rhythm of your heartbeat. What does your highest potential look like? Paint the canvas of your life with dreams turned into reality: no more comparisons, no more doubts—only the fierce determination to create a life by design, fueled by the fire within. Your mind arrives before you do.

Action

Take bold action.

In the midst of the action, dreams take flight. Your hopes, your aspirations—they demand activation. Set your GPS in life and embark on the journey towards your brightest future: no more hesitations, no more second-guessing. Turn your drafts into reality, for the heat of action creates transformation. Declare, "I can. I will. I am."

You are the firekeeper of your destiny. Don't let your flame go out and give up; instead, tend to it with care and watch as you illuminate the path to greatness. Remember, your fire is not yours alone to tend. Celebrate all our fires, for together, our collective Light will shape a better world for generations.

Author Bio

Nicole Scheffler

With a tech career spanning about 20 years, Nicole Scheffler has established herself as a Tech Diva. Her journey began in programming at a startup before she transitioned through various engineering roles at Cisco Systems for 15 years and worked a short time at VMWare. She is currently a Solutions Director at Palo Alto Networks, a renowned cybersecurity company.

With a passion for empowering women, Nicole serves women through her Tech Diva Success collection. She is a prolific author, publishing four Best-Selling books and over 160 podcasts. She co-founded the Diva Tech Talk podcast in 2015 with Kathleen Norton-Schock, which has received eight awards. The podcast captures the diverse career journeys of tech divas. Motivated by this initiative, Nicole established Tech Diva Success, which offers various modalities for empowerment. She is a sought-after speaker who has graced hundreds of stages, addressing topics ranging from technology to mindset, and she is a certified success coach. She offers a wealth of resources tailored for divine, inspired women with a rich vision, ready to take action in their lives and careers. She believes we all have innate gifts and should invest in self-care.

Nicole is deeply committed to philanthropy, dedicating her time to initiatives supporting women and the homeless. An avid explorer of future technologies, she loves live music and adventures with her family.

• TechDivaSuccess.com

This chapter is dedicated to my five brilliant, capable, independent and accomplished children. (Yes. I am proud) Some of my greatest leadership lessons came from learning to be their mother.

Leading by Lifting Others

Marva Sadler

"Ultimately, leadership is not about glorious crowning acts. It's about keeping your team focused on a goal and motivated to do their best to achieve it, especially when the stakes are high and the consequences really matter. It is about laying the groundwork for others' success, and then standing back and letting them shine."

- Chris Hadfield - former NASA Director of Operations, winner of the Order of Canada and the NASA Exceptional Service Medal, and Best-Selling Author

Chris Hadfield's leadership philosophy is as simple as it is radical: great leaders ensure team cohesion, empower employees by encouraging their growth, and then move aside to let their people lead. There are six key elements to this philosophy that I rely upon. They are:

1. **Keep the Team Focused on the Goal:** *Every significant success comes from a cohesive team whose members are willing to set aside individual objectives in favor of the larger, shared objective.*

Early in my executive journey, I assumed leadership of the back-office operations of a large corporate training company. The team included eight directors spread over five offices. Each of the eight was responsible for a different function. These functions were centralized from four divisions that operated independently for many years. The consolidation caused power struggles among vice presidents, resulted in significant job cuts, and destroyed long-standing friendships. The back-office operations became a target for political interference and maneuvering from unhelpful executives. The consolidation's original creator was removed for failure to deliver promised results.

I was given one mandate by my new boss: make the operations functional within six months.

I encountered a team in disarray. Amidst floundering operations, all four divisions demanded a return to their former autonomy. Organizing an intensive summit gave us the focus we needed. We identified core improvements to team dynamics and reestablished a clear mission and purpose.

With clarity and a shared vision, we renewed our work. Two directors who refused to give up their turf battles had to go. The remaining core team became remarkably productive, cohesive, and highly successful. Division executives who were pleading to return to "the old ways" cited the positive atmosphere being created and began hosting planning meetings in our offices.

A few years later, when the company was acquired, the consolidated back office had become a highly performing, cohesive unit. The acquiring company replaced its own support operations and embraced the model we had built. The success of this consolidation was founded on the achievements of the 200 team members whose jobs we saved. And the leaders all went on to greater opportunities and successes.

   2. Don't Wait! Motivate: *Bad morale is contagious. So is good morale. Great leaders determine which condition the team experiences.*

The Director's Summit helped immensely, but there were more challenges. Over 1200 internal customers had endured such bad Tech Support experiences that, understandably, they began bypassing the helpdesk entirely. Instead, they complained directly to their division VPs (copying me), expressing their bitter dissatisfaction with how technical issues were handled. The constant stream of complaints severely demoralized the helpdesk team: we were risking a mass walkout.

This negative culture had to change – fast. I enlisted the support of every VP and Director throughout the company, inviting them to let me know when they encountered great service. I printed out each email I received and penned a personal note to the individual recognized for doing something right. I included a small star-shaped magnet with the words "customer service star."

The impact was profound.

The first recipient of a note displayed the magnet proudly on his cubicle, sparking a trend among the team. Initially, complimentary emails trickled in, but they did come. Slowly, the defeated attitude within the helpdesk began to change. Team members began going the extra mile in efforts to earn a star. The trickle became a river. Eventually, a flood of positive comments poured in each week. The helpdesk team began competing to see who could collect the most stars. I had to order more stars.

The transformation was dramatic.

Customer service improved. Customer satisfaction increased significantly. The boost in team morale was tangible and measurable. People who came to our offices for management meetings would stop by the helpdesk to chat with their favorite tech and, in the process, would get their computers tuned up. Building on this momentum, the helpdesk manager created a new service – cleaning up every salesperson's computer while the salesperson attended the quarterly sales meeting. The initiative was wildly successful and saved the company over half a million dollars.

All this because of a little recognition and a fifty-cent magnet.

3. High Stakes Require Laser Focus: *Energy spent worrying about a problem is wasted. Focus on the solution and give it everything you have.*

The stakes couldn't have been higher when the tech consulting firm I served as CFO faced an imminent shutdown due to a critical cash shortage. A new customer became our biggest client, accounting for 20 percent of monthly revenue. We hired several additional experienced consultants to meet their specific demands. The client's promise of additional projects and a long-term relationship lulled the sales team into complacency in generating new accounts. However, there was a major problem. The client was slow to pay.

Despite personal assurances from the client's CEO, no payments were made. Eventually, this customer's debt rose to 10 percent of our annual revenue. And we faced a harsh reality. The client finally admitted that it could pay nothing. They were out of funds. Additionally, we had exhausted our credit line waiting for payment. With less than 30 days' operating cash flow and without the client's business, we were operating at a loss, with no prospects in the pipeline.

This could have become the beginning of a downward spiral that triggered layoffs of our best consultants, our vendors going unpaid, and a looming shutdown of our operations. But it didn't.

Rather than succumbing to despair, we rallied the team and put together an emergency plan to confront the challenge head-on. We set weekly targets for what we needed to accomplish to cover the losses. We reported our progress daily to the entire team: every success and every setback, as well as how much more we needed to do to get back to profitability. Every possible avenue was explored to generate revenue: We negotiated early project extensions, reached out to former clients, and accepted work that we would have declined previously.

Throughout the crisis, the team displayed unwavering focus, commitment, and determination. We pulled off something close to a miracle: within 30 days, we achieved breakeven. Within 60 days, we were paying back our loans. Not all the projects we accepted in that period were exciting or innovative, but they safeguarded jobs and saved the company. In just 90 days, we were back on solid ground, allowing us to be more selective about the clients we would take on in the future.

What stands out during this challenging time is the exceptional engagement from every team member. We achieved the seemingly impossible, saving every consultant's job and rescuing the company from the brink of collapse. We did so by pulling together. It was a testament to the power of unity and determination when the stakes are high.

4. Purpose is Paramount: *When we focus on what matters most, everything else aligns and makes sense.*

Researchers tell us that Millennials and Gen Zs place significant emphasis on Purpose in their work. They care about more than just financial gain or shareholder value. They want to be part of something meaningful that contributes to the world beyond the present moment.

As CEO of a leading coach education company, our clear Purpose was to "Raise the Global Standard of Coaching." During recruiting, we selected candidates who knew how to embrace this Purpose over specific experience or skill sets. We emphasized our Purpose in our job descriptions, and during our interviews, we looked for talent who aligned with that goal. This approach attracted dedicated and motivated individuals who resonated with our mission.

Every time we deviated from this principle to focus on skills or experience over Purpose, we regretted it. We invariably lost that person to poor performance, bad fit, or lack of commitment within a few months. EVERY. SINGLE. TIME. On the other hand, when we took a chance on a candidate who aligned with our Purpose but had less experience than desired or appeared to lack skill, the candidate succeeded and became an integral part of the team.

Junior Program Coordinators became adept Program Directors and E-Learning Architects and Partnership Development Managers. Mid-level website developers who lacked the level of experience of others nevertheless found innovative ways to enhance our technical infrastructure, reduce website development time, and improve system reliability.

Identifying and upholding Purpose is central to everything the organization does. It serves as a driving force to attract the right talent, nurture their growth, and propel the organization to greater success. It needs to be ingrained in the hearts and minds of every individual within the organization. When team members understand and connect with the Purpose, mundane tasks take on greater meaning. Creativity and problem-solving skills grow, and individuals and teams become deeply committed to achieving the Purpose. This leads to remarkable outcomes that positively impact the organization and the larger world.

5. Nurture Others' Success: *The leader's primary function is to help others tap into their full potential.*

Skills development aligned with Purpose doesn't happen by chance. It requires thoughtful leadership and intentional professional development. Junior Program Coordinators can become successful Program Directors as a consequence of an intentional approach that combines the individual's skills and desire to grow with the leader's dedication to helping each team member succeed. As an example, a talented Program Coordinator expressed concern that he wasn't being encouraged by his director to develop. I committed to him that if he would work with me on his professional development, we would chart a path that led to significant additional responsibility. Within two years, he was promoted three times and became a Program Director. He was valued as a senior member of the leadership team and became recognized as a program expert and an exceptional performer.

An effective leader understands the strengths of each team member and empowers each to transform those strengths into superpowers. The process involves much more (and much less) than merely giving the right answers and offering compliments. It demands time and a willingness to challenge team members to identify issues and propose solutions.

Good leaders listen to the ideas of their people and help refine them so they can withstand the pressures of real-world challenges. Rather than spoon-feeding answers, leaders guide individuals in seeking answers and evaluating potential solutions. It's about teaching them to think critically and independently and giving them opportunities to implement their ideas and practice those newfound capabilities in a supportive environment. Crawl...walk...run.

6.   Stand Back and Let Them Shine: *It's not enough to share credit when sharing credit is due. Great leaders actively create opportunities for their team members to experience and bask in the limelight.*

As the new CFO of a different global training company, I encountered a serious financial challenge. The training division operated without a budget, lacked performance targets, and suffered from a lack of trust in departmental cost reports. This situation posed significant difficulties for the financial function.

The finance team was without leadership for some time. They were demoralized and discouraged. Every solution they suggested was ignored. Without a leader, they had little influence in key decision-making or process development. As a group, we identified the core issues and the obstacles to implementing solutions. Accounting accuracy was suspect. Department managers were unsophisticated about financial issues, and decision-making was decentralized. We needed a solution that addressed all the challenges simultaneously without overwhelming the managers or distracting them from their other responsibilities.

A young, proactive financial analyst approached me with a proposal. He suggested that team members meet with each cost center manager every month to review their reports in detail. They did this diligently for three months, meticulously identifying inconsistencies in any cost account that didn't make sense to the manager. They researched each discrepancy and established new processes to resolve the underlying issues. They discovered a significant underlying issue: managers were charging expenses to other departments when they didn't want their spending reflected in their accounts. There were no controls or approval processes in place.

Soon, the monthly financials became clean and accurate. The team returned to the department managers to review past spending patterns. They collaboratively created budgets for the next year. Although the process was painstaking and time-consuming, it created credible financial reports and a well-structured budget for the first time in the division's history. This newfound financial clarity meant managers were held accountable for their spending. The result was a $2 million cost reduction in the first year.

In an executive meeting, the CEO commended me for the improvement in both process and outcome. I, in turn, gave credit to the analyst and his leadership on the project. The CEO's response was a masterclass in good leadership: he declared emphatically that having a team that can take initiative and improve systems was exactly what he wanted.

Giving credit to the analyst led to his promotion and a well-deserved raise. This outcome naturally motivated the entire finance team to work harder to identify additional improvements. They now knew that effective improvements would be adopted and – just as importantly – that they would be acknowledged for outstanding work.

This experience highlighted the power of initiative, creativity, and teamwork. Moreover, the role that genuine recognition plays in fostering continuous improvement, accountability, and team morale was unmistakably on display for every employee – every potential new leader – to see.

Transformational leadership in business and community means recognizing that a leader's responsibility is to serve and shape others. One leader can make a difference by moving ego aside in favor of encouraging the growth and accomplishments of their team. Our greatest satisfaction will come from celebrating the moments when a team member develops a better solution, a more creative idea, or an improved process.

Exceptional leaders understand that their greatest contribution may be in developing the people who will take the team, department, or organization to new heights and establish new standards of excellence. They create opportunities for their people to "stand on the shoulders of giants," and then they quietly stand back and let them shine.

Author Bio

Marva Sadler

Ms. Sadler is Managing Director of MLSOdyssey LLC, specializing in consulting to small businesses. She is an experienced business executive and consultant with over 20 years leading strategic and operational growth programs for organizations large and small. Her most recent corporate positions were as COO of Coaching.com, and CEO of WBECS, The World Business and Executive Coach Summit.

She's also held executive positions (EVP, CFO, and CEO) in large organizations, including Franklin Covey, and Achieve Global, and worked across a wide variety of industries, including professional services, software development, commercial fitness equipment manufacturing, car dealerships, and wool blanket manufacturing (in a historic woolen mill).

Marva began her career in strategy consulting with global strategy firm Bain and Co. She has also served in the nonprofit sector as Program Director for People Helping People, an employment success program for low-income women, and as a Board Member and strategic advisor for No More Homeless Pets of Utah. Marva is a certified Theory of Constraints Jonah.

- linkedin.com/in/marva-sadler/
- marvasadler@gmail.com

And yet... She Persisted

Betsy Rosenberg, *aka Woman on E-mission*

Over the years, I've learned—the hard way—about an area of professional focus where it does not pay to be first or even an early leader. It's the environment, or as I prefer to say, "our environment," since we all need to be much better stewards.

Unfortunately for me, I chose that specialty. Or rather, it chose me. Little did I know, nearly 30 years ago, when I launched a "green beat" on the radio station where I worked as a reporter, how long it would take for the media and public to recognize the value of content focused on eco-solutions. In retrospect, hundreds of environmentally focused shows later, I became an accidental trailblazer in my industry—broadcast news.

To understand how I became an unlikely green pioneer in media, I must go back to my childhood. Call me weird, but when I was growing up, waste always bothered me. I couldn't understand why wasting perfectly good food, water, or electricity didn't irk others, too. It felt like I was born with an extra chromosome, a green gene, that most "normal people" didn't possess. I've spent nearly three decades waiting for the world—and the news business—to catch up.

Earlier in my journalism career, I wouldn't have considered myself to be exemplary, though I landed a network job in my early 30s. I'd never aspired to be a national correspondent, but my job as a reporter for KCBS Radio in San Francisco led me to a network anchor position in New York.

In this brief overview of turning points in my career, I hope to show how serendipity, vision, perseverance, and a personal peeve-turned-full-blown-passion led me to where I am today.

Most of my professional career was spent with CBS Radio, and while the on-air role was impressive to others, it never felt like my heart was in it. Covering breaking news had its exciting moments—and appealed to my ADHD need for novelty—but it got old after a few years and exhausting after a decade. I yearned for something more purpose-driven.

Following my marriage and the birth of our daughter, I decided not to return to being a general reporter. My husband Alan helped me find my true passion: becoming a trash lady! Not exactly a garbage woman, but I did recycle my career.

Early in our marriage, I shared—not only a bathroom sink with my hubby—but also my distaste for waste. Growing up in New York, Alan wasn't exposed to droughts and the need to conserve water as I was in California. So when he ran the water while shaving or brushing his teeth, I would make "a-hem" sounds until he learned to turn it off. Little did he know that was only the beginning of living with who he called the Martha Stewart of Waste.

Alan's "education" unwittingly became the impetus for my mission. As I was deliberating how to use my broadcast experience and nose for news in a way that didn't involve covering depressing daily dramas, Alan helped me see I could create green content to run on KCBS Radio and spread awareness and action (and guilt). That would also take my focus and pressure off of him!

And so, it began...my recycled career. Launching on Earth Day, 1997, my 60-second *TrashTalk* segments offered ways to reduce, reuse, recycle, and rot (compost). I included soundbites from waste prevention experts and was entirely in my element—openly expressing my "green gene" and finding kindred spirits along the way!

When I first pitched my news director a feature about waste, he laughed. Originally, I wanted to call the segments *Waste Watchers*, but he was afraid *Weight Watchers* would come after me (hah, I *wish* since that would have been great publicity :). He predicted I'd have enough material for a three-week run. A decade later, I retired *TrashTalk* and, along the way, expanded into doing a one-hour interview program called *EcoTalk*, and widened my scope from garbage to global warming.

The shows ran on Air America Radio for three-and-a-half turbulent years between 2004-2007. It was a short-lived "liberal" network where Rachel Maddow made her broadcasting debut. One of us went on to TV fame and fortune!

Although my green show took me into the red financially, I was hopelessly committed by then (as I often say only half-jokingly, "Someday I may *end up committed*" because of my stubborn perseverance). The more I learned from my expert guests, the more hooked I became, convinced I was on to something BIG.

How could such important developments—impacting nothing short of our human survival—not be topping the news on mainstream networks or even appearing in major newspapers? I quickly fell in love with my self-appointed, self-funded beat. But for too many years to follow, I wondered why more journalists weren't covering this most compelling area of focus. Maybe they just lacked that extra green gene.

In 2007, after Air America declared bankruptcy—crashing my significant investment with it—I took a year off to recover. In addition to all the money expended in production costs—and what I was forced to pay the network to run my cutting-edge, popular programs—I needed to heal from the twin traumas of realizing the climate, ocean, extinction, etc., crises were worsening, just as my prospects for finding a stable and sustainable media platform looked dim. The recession had begun, and seemingly nobody wanted to hear about *my brand of green.*

The deep disappointment I felt about my industry's lack of interest in the hard-won eco-expertise I cultivated would be repeated over and over for the next two decades (and counting). I pitched—or *tried* to pitch—each of the television news networks on a show I titled "Meet the Solutionaries," where I interviewed eco-innovators who have an abundance of knowledge and passion to share on *all shades of green.* We desperately need their wisdom, yet programming executives could not have been less interested! They viewed environmental content as a niched subject area, not of high general interest. Well, maybe they just don't know HOW to MAKE it interesting!

Although my audience testimonials reflected an ability to make complex and often difficult subjects engaging and even entertaining, it didn't seem to matter to the networks. They were closed-minded, timid, and unable—or unwilling—to consider the opportunity to break new ground on an untapped area of focus while doing some public good. It's only humanity hanging in the balance!

If my show was a hit on radio 20 years ago, I can only imagine the impact today, now that the world is finally waking up to smell the carbon. I never had a budget for marketing my program, so it was all word of mouth, or as I say—it grew organically. I went on to do an Internet radio show for six years, but it was unpaid and had an audience limited by my ability to pay for help promoting it. I drew satisfaction in knowing I was helping to get publicity for my guests' causes, campaigns, events, programs, policies, books, films, you name it—if it was green, I was game to promote it!

What I *did* gain by interviewing hundreds of green experts was a high Eco-IQ. Between my recorded conversations and attending dozens of conferences each year—from Zero Waste to Zero Emissions—I learned so much from individuals I hold in high regard.

Over those years, I had some big wins, but it was all behind the scenes and benefitted others, so that may have to be my quiet legacy. In addition to convincing Jeff Zucker that CNN needed a climate correspondent—which prompted him to promote Bill Weir, who was already on staff, to that very position—I have other green feathers in my cap. Among them is Van Jones, a community activist and organizer, who, I gave the name *Green Collar Jobs* when I interviewed him in 2005. He used it as the title for his book, which got the attention of the Obama administration, which led to his getting hired as the Green Jobs Czar, which then led to a commentator position at CNN!

Additionally, in 2017, I interviewed Trammell S. Crow in Dallas at his newly launched EARTHx. Crow is a rare breed, a Republican billionaire who happens to also be a passionate environmentalist. He's quite a character and I respected his efforts to create a bi-partisan event. That's why I suggested going beyond Texas by starting an EARTHx TV channel. Four years later, he did. Too bad he forgot where the idea came from!

I've always been inspired by people who focus on issues that have a broader impact beyond themselves or their families—the folks devoting their lives to making a positive impact. I especially revere environmental leaders because there is so little pay and recognition associated with educating the population despite the huge public benefit.

For too long, those working to protect nature, wildlife, and biodiversity—in essence, people and the planet—have been marginalized. I've long referred to this as the "green bias" in corporate newsrooms and American society in general.

The irony is we're motivated by a special interest—what I call *a very special* interest—to conserve the biosphere that makes ALL life possible. Sadly, we're being proven right, along with the scientists who have increasingly urgently predicting ecosystem collapse. But no one expected the arrival of climate change to come so swiftly and severely.

And yet...there is still NO program on any news network focused on our planetary pickle and what to do about it, which is mind-bending to me (beyond boggling). How can it be we are heading toward a climate cliff—and fast—yet the so-called news leaders don't see their roles as including solutions to our existential crises in their programming? Or, as one arrogant exec at CNN told me, "Sorry, but the environment is just not on our slate." Well, buddy, there aren't any good slates on a bad planet or good *anything* for that matter!

It's been more than a bit crazy-making over the years to have my inbox fill up with increasingly dire environmental news AND real-world solutions but not be able to share them with the greater public.

I've become convinced—based on my direct experiences—that there is collusion in corporate media to not properly cover the need for mass action with appropriate urgency. I've been forced to come to the sad and depressing conclusion the news gate-keepers do not want someone like myself (who knows too much) hosting and co-producing content, programs that would tell the truth about our ecological poly-crises and connect the dots with a relentless focus on solutions. This is why I *still* say it's the only sector where experience doesn't get you ahead!

As to why that is, you'll have to read my upcoming book-in-progress, but suffice it to say telling the truth must involve challenging capitalism's business-as-usual, endless growth model in the U.S. and elsewhere. If we're going to transition to renewable energy and a green economy at the speed necessary, we must look at the systems that got us here and what needs to change.

Despite all the rejection, disappointment, frustration, and setbacks accompanying being an unwitting green media ground-breaker, I have persisted. And now I'm a grandmother! My daughter, who was two years old when I began this journey, turns 30 this year.

What is my ultimate vision? With more challenges, solutions, and "solutionaries" than ever, I'm convinced the only way to have the impact needed is to build a 24/7 Green News Network or GNN. What could be more important and relevant than how we can save nature and, thus, ourselves? The climate, oceans, wildlife, rainforests, and beyond need our immediate attention!

Preserving the planet--and people—is not a spectator sport. It'll take all of us to cut our emissions in half by 2030, and we may not make it. But if I have my way, it won't be due to ignorance.

After two decades of trying but failing to convince the news networks that they can be heroes and have a lasting impact by spotlighting the kind of program(s) I envision, I'd love nothing more than to show them what they've been missing in their coverage.

While they have gotten over their aversion to saying the words "climate change" and sometimes do so in connection with extreme weather events *in real time*, they're only reporting the tips of the melting icebergs.

So what's next for me? I've decided, not without some reluctance, to scale back my vision and ambition. If I were in my 30s instead of my 60s, I would continue to chase my big green dream. But alas, life teaches us we have limits in time, energy, and different priorities as we age. Mine now are to enjoy life with my husband and family.

Each time I see my adorable granddaughter's smiling face, I feel a love so deep—but it's also tinged with trepidation about what her future might bring—that I vow to fight on while I still can.

After all, I'd hate to waste my expertise and collection of contacts accrued over more than two decades. And waste is what got me hooked on this quest, or as I call it, my gateway drug!

I've always seen myself as a communications bridge connecting the eco-experts to the wider public who needs the information and inspiration critical to making change happen. I have re-formed with a smaller group of volunteers and am calling the brand "Green Bridge Media."

So, how have my experiences—both personal and professional—led to life lessons and advice I can share with you? I'll sum it up in a few points:

If you're fortunate enough to choose your career path and have a passion, find a way to work it into your profession. By not ignoring my "green gene" and distaste for waste, I created something uniquely mine to offer the world. The same is true if there is something that doesn't yet exist but should: create it, and if there's a need, the demand will follow—even if it takes nearly three decades for the world to catch up :)

There will always be obstacles in your path, especially if you're breaking new ground, as I did with the nation's first daily green show. If your vision hasn't wavered, even if it needs tweaking, keep it in sight!

In the end, you'll either get or create your dream "job," or you'll have the satisfaction of knowing you tried and did your best.

I'll close by sharing a recurring thought I've had over the last few turbulent years. I believe it's time to turn over the reins to women leaders to run companies, communities, and countries.

With the world growing messier and more dangerous each day, it's time to "womanifest" positive change and turn the eco-tide before we commit eco-cide. Give us a decade and see what we can do. Even the smart men in my life agree it's time...it's past time!

And if you happen to know or meet someone who agrees this precious planet is worth preserving and recognizes the need to get much more of the public involved, please send them my way. Your kids and grandkids are counting on it and will thank you someday. And so will I. It truly is now or never—and later is too late.

Author Bio

Betsy Rosenberg

Betsy Rosenberg is a three-decade trailblazer in environmental journalism, forging a path in broadcast media long before there were any programs or podcasts exclusively dedicated to green topics.

After a successful on-air career with CBS Radio, Rosenberg left to "recycle" her career, using her reporting expertise and anchoring skills to focus exclusively on solutions to our ecological challenges. After conducting more than 5,000 interviews with leading environmentalists, Rosenberg has amassed archives and cultivated connections in the green community unmatched by anyone in the industry.

Along the way Betsy was trained by Vice President Al Gore for his Climate Reality Project, and has been a keynote speaker and moderator at dozens of sustainability conferences. In 2002 she co-founded a "Gasroots" educational campaign called *Don't Be Fueled: Mothers for Clean and Safe Vehicles* and met with top officials at GM to encourage them to produce hybrid and electric family-friendly SUVs and vans.

In 2021 Betsy was asked to lead GreenTV.com, an online video platform featuring interviews with leading "solutionaries." In 2024 she left to focus on writing a book about "Climate Collusion" focused on the 20-year period that mainstream media outlets - primarily news networks - engaged in a "dereliction of duty" by giving short shrift to the worsening climate crisis. That silence cost critical time that should have been spent educating and engaging the greater public.

By telling the truth, connecting dots most fail to see, and focusing on solutions--decades before corporate media companies were paying attention to these critically important existential threats—Betsy has blazed a trail with lasting impact.

• linkedin.com/in/betsy-rosenberg-b07495123/

Rising Ready:
Embracing Unexpected Opportunities for Creating Transformational Impact

Dr. Rebecca Niemeyer Rens

"No one who puts a hand to the plow and looks back is fit for service in the Kingdom of God."

- Jesus, *Luke* 9:62, *Bible, New International Version*

'Climb up! We'll teach you how to build a road." Hesitating only briefly, I clambered up a welded ladder and over the steel crawler track system of the 30-ton piece of heavy equipment. I stepped onto an elevated catwalk that spanned the entire width of the machine. I followed the narrow metal pathway over the belly pan filled with a thick web of hydraulic hoses, ultimately positioning myself onto a podium in the middle. This spot was designed to provide a clear view of the entire street paving operation and surrounding areas so an operator could effectively control the machine. From that position on top, I was at the pinnacle of the road-building process. I had a 360-degree view of how our company's people, materials, and machines would work together to create infrastructures that would build economies over the next few decades and improve the quality of life in many communities. At that moment, I was offered an opportunity to 'put a hand to the plow' by participating in a unique and unconventional role that enabled me to be a catalyst for changing leadership and perceptions in our local industry and community.

Take Advantage of Unexpected Opportunities

This pivotal point of personal significance in our work and, consequentially, in broadening industry and community ideologies occurred about ten years after starting a concrete construction business. At the beginning of that season, we had a new slip-form paving machine delivered to a job site. The machine symbolized our company's commitment to diversify from commercial and residential jobs into industrial municipal infrastructure projects. The purchase represented a major financial investment for our small firm, and we were aware it would alter the work and trajectory of our organization. Although I felt apprehensive, I understood that businesses fail when leaders become content and neglect to continuously develop their people and their outputs. I passionately believed that we had been called to take this leap of faith and that we had to leave behind some of the old products and service areas that had grown stale and lacked the profit margins we had initially experienced. This new acquisition was intended to be a catalyst for change, strategically pushing our organization into new areas of growth and diversification. And so, despite the opinions and expectations of conservative locals and industry professionals, I became a functioning female in the concrete construction industry.

That day, I was on the job site hoping to capture the launch with photos to be posted on our website. The sun was just up and over the hills surrounding the small rural community where we had secured one of our season's first street paving projects. Crew members were busy making sure the string line was set correctly and that shovels, trowels, and floats were available and well-positioned. Conditions were ideal for pouring concrete. I was in blue jeans and work boots, a travel mug of hot black coffee in my hand, an early spring breeze was fresh on my face, the smell of hot oil and diesel exhaust scented the air (believe me – it grows on you), and our new concrete paving machine was unloaded onto the dirt grade.

Paving days were always a little stressful, but it was an exciting morning, filled with a nervous energy you could feel as everyone hustled around. It occurred to me as I watched that each person knew their job and was valuable and important in making the day's concrete pour a success. As I stood on the side of the dirt path that would become a road, I was grateful for the crew God had given us and the gifts, talents, and work ethic they supplied our company. I did not realize then that I would have the privilege of working shoulder-to-shoulder with these men and that I would get to become an instrumental part of this team.

Three male representatives from the machine manufacturer were also on-site that morning to get the machine set up correctly and provide training. We soon realized we had not hired a designated operator for this machine. While we had good people, no one on our current crew was equipped and available to fill that role. So, when we realized there was a gap, I climbed up on the machine, and they trained me. I do not recall their names, but I remember these men did not seem to care that I was a woman. They got busy showing me how to manipulate the machine's steering and speed, augers, tamper bars, and belts. I learned about spreading ready mix, working the materials, filling curb molds, and optimizing the finish of our product. It never occurred to me that this work was something I could not or should not do because of my gender.

That day, I could have backed away from the chance to participate. I could have adhered to norms and opinions that claimed building roads was a man's job. But, that choice would have delayed the entire crew's training and the owner's progress on the project. It would have cost our corporation a significant amount of time and money while trying to acquire an experienced operator. It also would have cost me the opportunity to grow in my industry understanding, experience, and leadership.

Let me encourage you not to step away—even when the opportunities are not what you anticipated or necessarily desired. Unexpected opportunities can often be catalysts for positive change. Embracing these types of occasions in non-traditional roles is not easy—it requires adaptability, resilience, and a growth mindset. However, if you are willing to think outside the box, navigate through unchartered territories, and explore unconventional options, it is very likely that you can experience exciting personal enrichment and professional growth just as I did.

Be Grateful for Support and Encouragement

For the next three seasons, in addition to being Owner and President, I was also the Machine Operator on paving days. In my experience, nothing elevates your relevance as a leader and motivates your people more than participating with them in the actual work performed.

Not only did my team members and material suppliers notice my participation, but the public also often came out to watch, snapping pictures of the "lady" running the heavy equipment. One day, an elderly woman waved me down from the controls. Although a little apprehensive, I took the opportunity while waiting for the material to arrive and climbed off the machine to find that she wanted to shake my hand and support me in my work. She explained that she served in the Women's Army Corps (WAC) during WW II and was one of the women who was instrumental in transforming perceptions of how females could serve their country. She just wanted to encourage me to change perceptions and break down barriers for women in the construction industry. I immediately felt an affinity for this gutsy and determined woman. I felt affirmed by her and supported and encouraged in my work as a member of a construction crew. She acknowledged me and my contribution. She helped me recognize that my work was about more than a new street – it was also about changing expectations for all women with a calling to work in non-traditional roles.

Deal with Issues, Don't Dwell on Them

My stint as a heavy equipment operator represented less than 10% of my time in the industry; however, it changed how I was able to contribute my passions and gifts as a business manager and leader. Stepping into that job and meeting that need greatly enhanced my ability to become a successful entrepreneur, empowering me to build a profitable business and contribute to the lives of my employees, their families, and surrounding communities. I knew I was answering a call for that season in my life, and I had unique capabilities to contribute. I was confident that, in the words of Dr. Sasha Shillcutt, "God made me a woman; instead of limiting myself in my own mind because I was not a man, I had to start accelerating myself internally because I was a woman" (Shillcutt, p. 50).

During those years, I made mistakes and encountered challenges. I was misunderstood, misrepresented, underestimated, subjected to inappropriate behaviors from people outside of my company, condescended to, and often isolated. There were days when bolts sheared off, augers or tamper bars got caught up under the machine, hydraulic hoses blew, and the curbs would not stand up. The truth is that not all days are good days, not every project goes as planned, not all people are supportive, and not every employee or project partner will be concerned about the best interests of your organization.

Experiencing these job site challenges and negative behaviors helped me develop an understanding of and capabilities for doing my job and dealing with people. They taught me that if I remained caught up and overly concerned with the perspectives and expectations of the current culture, I would not be able to participate in the positive transformative change that was needed. I learned from the hard days that *it is wise to become better equipped to perform the tasks you control and more adaptable to the circumstances and elements you do not.*

I'm not suggesting that anyone tolerates being poorly treated; our goal should be to alter the culture so that those who come after us find an improved environment. However, I want to encourage you to address issues and move on – do not allow negativity to become an obsession. Being consumed by offenses will steal your energy and keep you from moving forward because, as Cathy Derksen has pointed out, adopting an attitude of victimhood inhibits your openness to new possibilities (Derksen). Instead, consider circumstances an opportunity for growth – deal with the issues as necessary but don't dwell on them.

Understand the Value of Doing the Work

I experienced many positive impacts because of being more engaged in the physical work of my company. Perceptions and levels of acceptance seemed to improve. I gained credibility and respect from my employees, fellow contractors, suppliers, owners, and engineers. I enjoyed and experienced what it is to be an integral part of a team. As Brene' Brown points out, "Daring leaders must care for and be connected to the people they lead," I found there is no better way to connect to those you lead than to work beside them. (Brown, p. 12)

People in the small local communities were still hesitant and slow to understand my behavior, but within my industry, there was a noticeable shift in attitudes toward me. By participating in a non-traditional position, I became better equipped to lead my company to success and became more respected for my abilities, as well as my grasp of industry knowledge and ethical practices. Those who underestimated me were caught off-guard when we started winning bids, and our company gained a reputation for high-quality products and services. My experience in the field provided me with invaluable knowledge about how our projects were built and about the processes and people necessary to complete the multi-million-dollar jobs we performed successfully. While much of my career was spent inside the physical walls of our organization, focused on the long-term strategies and practices for the success of our small business, briefly being part of the paving crew allowed me to engage in some of the shorter-term activities and projects that contributed to our overall goals.

Let Go and Look Up

Recent journal articles claim the percentage of women in construction and other male-saturated industries is on the rise. Additionally, research indicates gender diversity drives profitability and helps resolve labor shortages. Author Deborah Smith Pegues concurs with the findings, noting the "importance of having both genders represented at the table for maximum productivity and profitability" and asserting that companies experience more success when they can utilize and capitalize on the inherent traits of both women and men. (Smith Pegues, p. 11) So, if God has called you to an unconventional position at work, embrace opportunities to participate with your male counterparts to improve outcomes. Many organizations exist to help address the unique challenges that confront women working and leading in non-traditional roles. I suggest you seek these out and consider also engaging in opportunities for mentoring and networking. If you do, I believe you can become instrumental and appreciated for the valuable contributions you will make to overall success.

Move Beyond the Machine

As noted, my tenure as a heavy equipment operator was relatively brief, but it was a stimulus for so much more. In the years that followed, I had the opportunity to serve our organization in multiple capacities, including Owner, President, Estimator, Accountant, Employer, HR Manager, and General Contractor. In addition to gaining decades of practitioner experience as a small business owner, I also took opportunities to upgrade my formal academic education. I returned to school as an adult learner and earned my MBA and, a few years later, my Doctor of Business Administration degree. With my Doctorate accomplished, I went on to serve as an Assistant Professor of Business at a university where I taught undergraduate and graduate-level business and leadership courses. Through this process, I realized I have a passion for community and equipping others to reach their full potential.

As my journey continues, my goal is to see businesses redeem their environments and embrace the truth that "men and women were created for partnership" in work, regardless of the type or industry. (Moore, p. xix) I seek to facilitate inclusive workplaces and enhance team performance by helping businesses equip women in non-traditional roles with tools and strategies to empower them for effective participation and leadership as they partner with male colleagues in collaborations that contribute to enhanced personal and organizational success. I strive to provide tangible knowledge, mentorship, and support. My desire is that women in unconventional roles will grow in life and leadership by letting go of personal limitations and insecurities, traditional norms and expectations, and biased and discouraging people. My hope is that they will embrace their unique talents and God's design for their work, rising ready to reach new levels of personal influence, achievement, and organizational impact.

"See, I am doing a new thing! Now it springs up; do you not perceive it?"
- Isaiah 43:19 New International Version

Notes

1. Brown, Brene, "Dare to Lead: Brave Work. Tough Conversations. Whole Hearts." P. 12 (New York: Random House, 2018)

2. Derksen, Cathy, "Midlife Awakening: 20 Women Share Inspiring Stories of Midlife Transformation" (Action Takers Publishing, 2023)

3. Moore, Carolyn, "When Women Lead: Embrace Your Authority, Move Beyond Barriers, and Find Joy in Leading Others" (Grand Rapids: Zondervan Reflective, 2022).

4. Shillcutt, Sasha K., "Between Grit and Grace: The Art of Being Feminine and Formidable," p.50 (Boca Raton: Health Communications, Inc., 2020)

5. Smith Pegues, Deborah "Lead Like a Woman: Gain Confidence, Navigate Obstacles, Empower Others," p.11 (Eugene: Harvest House Publishers, 2020)

Author Bio

Dr. Rebecca Niemeyer Rens

Rebecca Niemeyer Rens is a former President, Owner, and General Contractor with over 30 years of leadership experience in the concrete construction industry. She has been personally involved with breaking down barriers and pursuing opportunities for women in male-dominated fields. As an educator and content creator, Dr. Rens has also served as an Assistant Professor of Business, Dissertation Chair, and Online Program Developer at multiple universities, designing and teaching business and leadership courses at both undergraduate and graduate levels.

Rebecca holds a Bachelor of Arts in Business Administration, an MBA, and a Doctor of Business Administration with a focus on Leadership. She is a DBA Graduate with Distinction and a member of the Delta Mu Delta International Honor Society in Business. Her doctoral research explored leadership adaptability in fast-changing, complex industry environments, and her findings have been published through Scholars Crossing and in a co-authored article in the Journal of Higher Education Theory and Practice.

Driven by a belief that God designed men and women for partnership in the workplace, Rebecca now draws on both her extensive first-hand experience and education to help women excel in male-saturated workspaces. She asserts women can thrive in non-traditional callings when they are empowered and equipped to contribute their best efforts; and organizations can fully leverage the diverse gifts and perspectives of their people when they intentionally foster harmony and collaborative environments.

- linkedin.com/in/rebeccaniemeyerrens

To my husband David, whose unwavering support and love fuel my dreams, and to my remarkable teachers, whose wisdom and guidance have shaped my journey—this chapter is a testament to your influence and inspiration. Thank you for everything.

Women in Entrepreneurship and Leadership:
Navigating Barriers and Cultivating Success From the Inside Out

Debbie Moore

'**The Before, During and After**' - A lived experience—journey into the challenges women face in leadership roles; actionable and sustainable strategies to overcome those challenges and develop and maintain the momentum to evolve.

Leadership Over the Years

Leadership theories and practices have traditionally been shaped by masculine experiences and developed in male-dominated contexts. Consequently, foundational ideas about leadership have often overlooked female leaders' unique challenges and styles. For decades, women have largely adapted to and excelled within a masculine framework of power, which emphasises logical, linear, and strategic thinking—characteristics associated with traditional notions of power as "to act, to accomplish, and to exert force."

While women have always held leadership roles, the systematic study of women's leadership is relatively recent. This emerging field examines how women lead, the barriers they face, and the distinct strengths they bring to leadership positions. Researchers and practitioners are working to understand what sets women's leadership apart and how societal structures may be adjusted to better support female leaders.

Current efforts focus on exploring how women's leadership diverges from traditional models and how best to support women in leadership roles by addressing structural barriers and societal biases. These challenges point to new opportunities for evolving leadership practices. Based on control and analysis, the traditional masculine system of power often falls short in addressing the complexities of modern leadership needs, resulting in underutilisation of the total talent pool and socio-economic consequences, as will be seen later.

Why is This Important?

Understanding and supporting women's leadership is crucial. For instance, McKinsey & Company reports that gender-diverse executive teams are 21% more likely to experience above-average profitability. Additionally, companies with higher female board representation see significantly higher returns on sales and invested capital.

According to The World Economic Forum, women entrepreneurs inspire other women to start businesses. This leads to more job creation for women, which ultimately helps communities and economies and reduces the gender gap in the workforce.

Studies have also found that an increased number of women in senior leadership positions improves overall employee engagement and retention bringing unique perspectives and experiences to decision-making processes, often leading to innovations and more collaborative and inclusive work cultures. This, in turn, boosts employee morale and productivity. Moreover, having women in leadership positions serves as role models for future generations.

Key Benefits of Women's Leadership:

1. **Diverse Perspectives:** Women bring innovative and effective solutions to business and society.
2. **Equity and Inclusion:** Supporting women's leadership creates environments where everyone can succeed.
3. **Maximising Talent:** Encouraging women's leadership maximises the potential of the entire talent pool.
4. **Economic Growth:** Women leaders drive better financial performance.
5. **Role Models:** Female leaders inspire future generations to pursue leadership roles.

In summary, while women's leadership is not new, the focused study and support of it are evolving. With more authentically empowered women in leadership positions, it's not just good for women—it's good for business and society.

This chapter builds on this premise, my own experience, my work with thousands of women globally, and published research. In this wider context, based on experience, my chapter is intended to contribute to women transforming leadership in business and the community by taking what, for some, could be a significantly different perspective. This includes seeking support and looking from the 'inside out,' embracing self-leadership, a growth mindset, and building authentic confidence. These are part of the essential tools for creating lives, work, and contributions in a women-centred paradigm.

A Personal Perspective

My journey has been far from straightforward. With over four decades in operational and leadership roles, transitioning from a corporate leader to a business founder, I've encountered common challenges many women leaders and entrepreneurs face. These include internal pressures often outside our conscious awareness, self-imposed and learned behaviours, as well as external pressures such as cultural norms, societal expectations, and biases.

Self-limiting beliefs like imposter syndrome, navigating relationship dynamics, conflict resolution, and maintaining work-life balance can hinder your potential and happiness. Reflecting on my experiences, I frequently struggled with internal pressures and the fear of 'not knowing,' leading to shame-based thinking. Often, I felt desperately unhappy and exhausted, questioning if this was all life had to offer.

A personal crisis, including divorces and a severe relationship betrayal, resulted in a loss of confidence and near-burnout, significantly impacting my health, life, work, and relationships. However, with focused support, I committed to addressing these challenges, starting with my growth. Tackling these intricate issues demanded collaborative action and innovative solutions.

Through continuous learning and leading in my own life, focusing on sustainable growth from the inside out, and sharing the insights and modalities that work, my intention is to contribute to building a more resilient, equitable, and prosperous world for current and future generations.

Building on my master's degree research in 2008, "The Role of the Body in Coaching and Mentoring Interventions," I explored how our physiology impacts our self-concept, reactions under pressure, behaviour, mood, and actions, influencing leadership and life. As the Founder of Embody Coaching Ltd., and with decades of experience, I embraced the opportunity to evolve both my life and my practice.

Inspired by my mentor and colleague, Dr. Claire Zammit, who researched the obstacles blocking intelligent, conscious women from stepping into their greatness, I specialise in supporting ambitious women in leadership and SMEs to overcome these hurdles, pursue their passions, live their dreams, and make a meaningful impact in the world.

I have since supported thousands of individuals on their growth journey, moving from fear to freedom in life and relationships—both personally and professionally.

A Wake-Up Call

In Autumn 2022, I found myself delivering an impromptu presentation to a group of accomplished leaders, entrepreneurs, and professionals. With nearly six decades of life behind me, I realised that the years ahead were likely fewer than those already lived. In that moment, without a prepared agenda, I spoke candidly from the heart about my ongoing inquiry into my purpose and contribution. I admitted that I didn't have the clear, concise introduction typically expected in such settings because, truthfully, I was still figuring it out.

Instead, I shared a reflection on the reality of feeling constrained—physically, mentally, or emotionally—by societal expectations and the pressure to always "say the right thing" or conform. I touched on past experiences of trying to fit in despite an inner sense of dissonance and moments where defensiveness or a feeling of being stuck prevailed. Yet, amidst this vulnerability, I offered a glimmer of hope—a reminder that it doesn't have to be this way. Using the skills I've garnered over decades; I spoke openly about exploring new possibilities to add value through my work.

After the presentation, a successful entrepreneur, whom I'll call Marie, approached me with eyes betraying a mix of exhaustion, confusion, and fear. Her plea for guidance echoed sentiments I had encountered in numerous successful professionals before her. As she poured out her heart, I empathised, recognising the familiar struggle of outward success coupled with inward despair and misalignment.

Curious, I gently probed into what's known as 'somatic' awareness and how, as women and leaders, we can move beyond what holds us back. This, in part, involves navigating the 'fight, flight, freeze, or please' responses to develop a more authentic, skilful, and embodied way of being. Yet, Marie's emphatic response revealed a glaring gap in my understanding.

This exchange wasn't isolated. It mirrored conversations I had with other successful leaders and entrepreneurs, highlighting recurring themes. This pivotal moment propelled me to share my insights in this chapter.

I recognise the prevailing wisdom often assumes an us-versus-them paradigm, pitting women against men. However, my intention is not to perpetuate this narrative. Instead, I aim to bring into conscious awareness the prevalent leadership challenges and insights I've encountered over decades as a corporate leader and as a life and leadership transformational coach and how we can begin to move beyond them—from the inside out.

So, What Does the Research Tell Us?

Key research findings, in the context of this chapter, highlight the challenges and opportunities for women in leadership roles:

1. **The Glass Ceiling and the Broken Rung:** While the term "glass ceiling" has long described the invisible barrier preventing women from reaching the highest leadership levels, recent insights from Forbes, McKinsey, and LeanIn.Org reveal a more pervasive issue known as the "broken rung." This term refers to the first critical step up to manager, where for every 100 men promoted, only 87 women achieve the same. This promotion gap starts early in women's careers, leading to a disproportionate number of men in middle management and, subsequently, more men ready for senior positions.

2. **Confidence Dynamics:** Research from the *Harvard Business Review* shows that confidence is often weaponised against women in leadership roles. Despite high levels of demonstrated confidence, women are perceived as lacking confidence, hindering their career progression. The GEM Global Entrepreneurship Monitor (GEM) 2023/2024 Global Report highlights the fear of failure as a significant barrier for women entrepreneurs. Despite recognising good opportunities, women are more likely than men to refrain from starting businesses due to this fear. Addressing confidence perception

biases is essential to empower women in their entrepreneurial pursuits.

3. **Identity Shift and Gender Bias:** CEOs who prioritise gender diversity often face challenges due to the fundamental identity shift required for women to see themselves and be seen as leaders. Second-generation gender bias, still prevalent in organisations, disrupts the learning cycle for aspiring women leaders. Overcoming this bias is crucial for creating inclusive environments where women can establish credibility and thrive.

4. **Feminine Power as a Tripartite System of Relatedness:** Dr. Claire Zammit's research on feminine power extends beyond gender, viewing the feminine as an archetypal principal present—or suppressed—in both men and women. This suppression has significant societal and global implications.

In summary, these research findings underscore the complex challenges women face in leadership and entrepreneurship, including confidence perception biases, identity shifts required for leadership, and persistent fears of failure. Addressing these challenges requires concerted efforts to educate about biases, create inclusive environments, and provide tailored support and resources, ultimately fostering gender diversity and empowering women to thrive as leaders and entrepreneurs.

A Double Bind for Women in Leadership Roles

This double bind refers to the conflicting expectations and pressures that women face, which can create further challenging dilemmas. Here are the key aspects of the double bind for women in leadership:

1. Expectations of Leadership Style & Cultural and Societal Expectations
Assertiveness vs. Likeability: Women leaders are often expected to be assertive and confident, qualities traditionally associated with effective leadership. However, when women exhibit these traits, they may be perceived as aggressive or unlikable. On the other hand, if they are collaborative and empathetic, they may be seen as too soft or not authoritative enough.

2. Perceptions of Competence

Performance Pressure: Women in leadership roles may face greater scrutiny and must continually prove their competence and capabilities. Mistakes or failures may be judged more harshly, both by themselves and others, compared to their male counterparts, reinforcing stereotypes about women's abilities in leadership.

3. Balancing Professional and Personal Roles

Work-Life Balance: Women leaders often navigate the additional pressure of balancing professional responsibilities with societal expectations related to family and caregiving roles. This can lead to heightened stress and the need to make difficult choices between career advancement and personal obligations. It's worth noting that calls for greater flexibility in this regard are growing from men as well as women.

4. Bias and Discrimination

Implicit Bias: Women leaders frequently encounter implicit biases that influence how they are perceived and treated. These biases can manifest in hiring, development, and promotion decisions, as well as in everyday interactions, limiting opportunities for women to advance and succeed in leadership roles.

In summary, the double bind for women in leadership involves navigating the conflicting expectations of being assertive yet likable, demonstrating competence while being scrutinised more intensely, balancing professional and personal roles, and overcoming cultural and societal biases.

These challenges require women leaders to continuously adapt and find a balance that enables them to lead effectively while managing the pressures and expectations placed upon them. In my experience and those I've worked with, sadly none of this is new.

Evolving Our Identity From the Inside Out – Unconscious Gaps

According to the *Harvard Business Review*, developing a leadership identity and a sense of purpose is a continuous journey shaped by intentional actions and influenced by how others react. These interactions significantly shape our self-perception as leaders or entrepreneurs.

Maslow's theory of self-actualization outlines the path towards realizing one's full potential, achieving personal growth, and fulfilling aspirations. Today, many women actively pursue this journey, striving to develop and express their capabilities to the fullest.

However, in her doctoral research on the underlying obstacles blocking intelligent, conscious women from stepping into their greatness, praised as a groundbreaking and seminal contribution to the advancement of women in this century, Dr. Claire Zammit identified a 'Power Paradox' phenomenon.

Despite being well-educated, talented, accomplished, and powerful, many women often feel under-realized and powerless to manifest their deepest aspirations and that the struggle is not our own fault or failure but "part of a much larger story of women awakening to their power."

To address this, a new paradigm—a Feminine system of power—emerges as essential. This system is intuitive, creative, and magnetic, enabling the creation and management of goals that cannot be achieved through strategic thinking alone. Recognising this shift, Dr. Zammit has developed research-based training to help women harness this Feminine power, which is essential for manifesting and creating at higher levels of self-actualisation.

The late Wendy Palmer's Leadership Embodiment somatic work emphasizes that our personalities are moulded by survival patterns. Recognizing these patterns is crucial in leadership development. Leaders must confront survival-driven behaviours like self-deception, which prioritize controlling outcomes over personal accountability. This shift from inward reflection to outward focus on others' behaviours can hinder genuine growth.

Bringing Unconscious Awareness Into Conscious Awareness: Overcoming Barriers and Harvesting Learning

Drawing on my experience supporting over a thousand individuals and the extensive research and insights from my mentors and colleagues, it's clear that effective entrepreneurship and leadership go beyond technical skills. This requires support, psychological safety, cultivating self-awareness, and relational and intuitive processes. To truly lead and create meaningful impact, the invitation is to connect with our ability to lead ourselves, cultivate a growth mindset, embrace inclusivity, and build authentic confidence.

To Lead Others Effectively, We Must First Lead Ourselves

The connection between self-leadership, a growth mindset, and authentic confidence is vital for personal and professional growth, especially for women leaders, so we can see our strengths, embrace vulnerability, and face challenges to harvest and learn with support.

1. **Self-Leadership:** Involves taking charge of one's life, making intentional choices aligned with personal values, and navigating challenges with resilience.

2. **Growth vs Fixed Mindset:** A growth mindset involves self-reflection to harvest key learning from our experiences, embrace the potential for improvement, fostering resilience and adaptability, essential for success.

3. **Authentic Confidence:** Grounded in self-awareness and self-acceptance, it requires recognising strengths, embracing vulnerability, and facing challenges with support and practice.

Strategies for Overcoming Barriers

1. **Recognise and Challenge Limiting Beliefs:** Address and transform limiting beliefs, such as imposter syndrome and fear of failure. For instance, Sally, a senior executive, overcame imposter syndrome by focusing on her vision and strengths, renewing her confidence.

2. **Develop Resilience Through Building Confidence:** Enhance resilience by setting boundaries and engaging in meaningful conversations. Emma, an entrepreneur, improved her well-being and relationships by mastering these skills, significantly boosting her effectiveness.

3. **Cultivate a Growth Mindset:** View setbacks as learning opportunities. Laura, a project manager, turned a major project failure into a chance for growth, enhancing her vision, collaboration skills, and significant commercial impact.

Conclusion

For women leaders and entrepreneurs, normalising shared experiences and addressing barriers is crucial. Engaging with a supportive network of peers, mentors, and coaches provides ongoing support for cultivating self-leadership, a growth mindset, and authentic confidence.

These elements are essential for overcoming challenges and achieving a fulfilling life. Prioritising well-being, balancing work and personal life, and setting boundaries are key to realising the path to self-actualisation. Embrace vulnerability, recognise strengths, and advocate for diversity and inclusion. By addressing these factors, we empower women to realise their full potential and drive positive, inclusive change in their lives and communities.

Author Bio

Debbie Moore

Debbie Moore is a distinguished expert in Woman-Centred Transformational Life & Leadership Coaching, with over 40 years of experience in facilitating meaningful change for individuals and organisations alike. As the founder of Embody Coaching Ltd, established in 2008, she has a proven track record of empowering clients to achieve transformative personal and professional growth.

An international best-selling author, award-winning coach, and respected speaker, Debbie partners with ambitious entrepreneurs and leaders on life-elevating journeys. Her impactful work has garnered global recognition, including an invitation to join the prestigious Coaching Faculty at The Institute for Woman-Centred Coaching. Additionally, she serves as an Associate Somatic Coach with Leadership Embodiment and a Support Partner with Women on Boards CIC.

Having positively impacted over 1,000 women worldwide, Debbie is known for her dedication and innovative methodologies, supporting clients to overcome challenges while cultivating the confidence, skills, and strategies necessary for sustained, extraordinary success in leadership, relationships, communication, and influence.

Holding an MSc in Coaching and Mentoring from Sheffield Hallam University and status as a Chartered Fellow of the CIPD, Debbie combines expertise with empathy in every partnership. Based in Leicestershire, UK, she shares a loving, fulfilling life with her husband, David Hayes, an Export Controls Expert, and remains passionately committed to facilitating lasting, transformative change.

Book your complimentary discovery session with Debbie today and explore how you can turn your aspirations into reality.

- debbie@debbiemoorecoaching.com

FullHearted Leadership

Bonnie Lynn

My Journey to FullHearted Leadership

In the cacophony of our daily lives, as women of experience and wisdom, we often find ourselves navigating the complex landscape of business and community leadership. We have been there and done that—wearing countless hats, striving to fit in, be heard, and care for everyone around us.

As seasoned professionals, we've amassed an impressive array of accomplishments and awards. Yet, within the depths of our being, nagging questions often persist: Have we truly reached our fullest potential? Isn't there more to life than what we've accomplished? This journey can leave us feeling fatigued, numb, and disconnected from our authentic selves.

I am intimately familiar with this journey. After co-founding and building a family-owned commercial construction company for over 25 years, I found myself at a standstill. Over the previous decade, I assumed the CEO role and grew our annual revenues from $1.8 million to $8 million. During this time, I also orchestrated the relocation and renovation of a sprawling 38,000-square-foot industrial warehouse that would become our headquarters.

As our business and pressures grew, so did the void within me. Despite external successes, I began to sense a growing emptiness—a yearning for something deeper, a longing for a profound connection with myself and others. Something I had been journaling about for decades but didn't know how to access despite my ever-growing shelf of self-help books. It was a call to become what I now have coined "FullHearted."

Unraveling On the Path to FullHearted Leadership

In the tumultuous year of 2020, we made the difficult decision to close our business. Simultaneously, a divorce after a four-decade-long marriage signaled the end of life as I knew it. I was in my second apartment, leaving behind the 20-acre hobby farm and family dream home I had designed. My circle of friends and family shifted dramatically. It was a painful and uncomfortable period.

Amidst these profound changes, I was also transitioning careers as I went about the process of closing out the business. My life was so uprooted that when the COVID-19 pandemic hit, despite the additional challenges, it actually provided the solitude and space I craved to reflect and simply be. I had lost everything society had painted as "The American Dream" for my generation.

Despite the magnitude of these changes, I possessed a gritty, unshakable resolve I had cultivated through years of navigating the male-dominated industry and facing life's ebbs and flows. I knew, in the end, I would be ok. My tenacity was rooted in survival, in a stubborn refusal to succumb to external pressures.

As I began crafting a new life on all fronts, I knew it had to be different. I knew I would have to be different. What had got me there would not get me to what was next.

In 2019, as I anticipated the inevitable shifts in my life's trajectory, I stumbled upon an opportunity to train with Dr. Claire Zammit. Her research-based findings, focused on self-actualization and uncovering the hidden barriers and inner glass ceilings that particularly plague women, resonated deeply within me. These teachings provided a stark contrast to the leadership styles and norms prevalent in the construction industry.

I wholeheartedly delved in, ultimately becoming a certified coach and founding member of Dr. Zammit's Institute for Women-Centered Coaching Leadership and Training.

By implementing these concepts, my life opened up in extraordinary ways, and I was able to powerfully meet each next step on my journey back to myself. There were micro-baby steps and bold leaps. I witnessed hundreds of other women having similar results.

Identifying Hidden Toxins – Clearing the Way for FullHearted Leadership

During my 25 years in construction, I endured an onslaught of unpleasantries, including bullying, threats, harassment, deception, bribery, and shaming. I was also forced to incur substantial financial losses so that the reputations of individuals and organizations in the power structure of traditional systems would remain unchallenged and without consequence—overt outbursts like name-calling, yelling, and gaslighting coexisted with intrinsic experiences of tokenization that quietly drained me. Even the patriarchy in the air of my own team and family festered and manifested in my body.

While the toll was immense, the most significant harm came from adopting the false narrative that I was failing as a leader, not likable, and a misfit in a man's world where someone else always had the upper hand. Despite the successes, recognition, and awards, there was no appeal in creating more of what I already had. I didn't want more of what I attributed to leaving me feeling depleted, stagnant, and dying on the inside.

In hindsight, I was trying to solve the wrong problem. I was stuck looking at all the external circumstances; the problem was the profound disconnection between myself and my own knowing. Conforming to achievement goal-based models and expectations seeped in outdated Status Quo ideals had robbed me of my innate wisdom, creativity, and zest.

From this realization emerged a ground-breaking question. What if the discontent and depletion women business leaders are experiencing stems from unmet potential rather than external circumstances?

I believe there are epic numbers of women leaders who are experiencing various levels of discontent camouflaging as originating from something else. So we are on a chase to relieve the discomfort, failing to recognize where it is coming from.

Lean In's Women in the Workplace 2022 Report says, "Women leaders are switching jobs at the highest rate we've ever seen." The report indicates it is increasingly important for women leaders to work for companies that foster employee well-being and inclusion.

The importance of fulfilling our highest potential is at the pinnacle of Maslow's hierarchy of human needs, yet conformity to succeed in business often stifles individual growth and expression. The consequences of trying to fit in – emptiness, stagnation, mental health challenges including anxiety and depression, and relationship strain – mirror those of genuine problems.

Cookie-cutter leaders lack the impact of those in tune with their genius. There is an opportunity to include self-actualization as a component of wellness and create the structures, cultures, and leadership development to encourage it. Once we uncover the hidden toxins within ourselves and our businesses, we can reconnect to our genuine essence to create out to the horizon line from that brilliance instead of looking out the rear-view mirror for direction.

The Responsibility for Transformation

While I acknowledge the challenges posed by a patriarchal and predominantly male-dominated industry, it is crucial to emphasize that women, myself included, cannot evade our share of responsibility. We are all accountable for fostering change. This does not entail placing sole blame on ourselves or granting excuses to others, nor does it involve tolerating the intolerable. I advocate for a candid examination of how we contribute to perpetuating hindrances, acknowledging our responsibilities, and actively disrupting detrimental patterns.

Even within boardrooms comprised entirely of women, I have observed divisive politics and personality conflicts that hinder progress and crush colleagues. What is imperative are new cultural norms and invincible growth containers that facilitate collective support over unhealthy competition, collaboration over scarcity, and prioritizing progress over pursuing unattainable perfection.

We need spaces where one individual's success does not diminish or invalidate another's accomplishments. These environments should empower us to shatter the self-imposed glass ceilings that live in our own psyches and unlock our true potential. It is time to reconnect with our authentic selves and allow our hearts to experience fullness once again. The responsibility lies with each of us to dismantle toxic behaviors and mindsets that hinder our growth and collective success.

The Birth of FullHearted Leadership

Poet Antonio Porcia says, "In a full heart there is room for everything, and in an empty heart there is room for nothing."

Looking back at my experience in the construction industry, I can see how the biases and challenges gradually disconnected me from my true self and the skills that initially empowered me. As my heart closed off, I lost touch with my unique essence, gifts, talents, and insights, which were the very qualities that had made me successful in the first place. It's fascinating how a full heart can bring us full circle.

FullHearted Leadership is not just about doing things differently; it's about being different. It's a transformative approach that commences with a profound shift—from mindsets grounded in the status quo, fear, and scarcity, often filled with biases and phobias, to mindsets centered on the boundless potential that emerges from a full heart and holds space for all.

FullHearted Leadership recognizes that individual change and self-connection serve as catalysts for collective change and vice versa; collective change is a catalyst for individual change. It thrives on the power of genuine relationships, empathy for the human experience, and the profound understanding that comes from the heart. A full heart empowers us to transcend fear, scarcity, biases, and phobias while recognizing the depth of our own and others' scars.

FullHearted Leadership revolves around harnessing our unique creativity, innovation, and untapped potential, which become accessible when we are deeply aware of and fully embrace our own genius—our personal fingerprint or signature. It requires a deep understanding of oneself, enabling us to connect with ourselves and with others authentically. This, in turn, leads to extraordinary and exponential results akin to a masterful symphony or a well-guarded recipe.

Hidden barriers and toxins are detrimental, creating gaps in our lives, leadership efforts, businesses, and communities. These gaps represent disparities between what we desire and what currently is. However, they also present hidden opportunities and untapped potential. Uncovering these gaps can reveal prime opportunities for change, problem-solving, and meaningful progress toward unity, wholeness, and connection within the framework of FullHearted Leadership.

Three Pillars of FullHearted Leadership

The heart, as it circulates blood in the body, serves three essential functions:
1. Remove Toxins from the Body (Filter)
2. Deliver Oxygen to the Body (Fill)
3. Deliver Nourishment to the Body (Fuel)

FullHearted Leadership is built on these same three fundamental pillars.

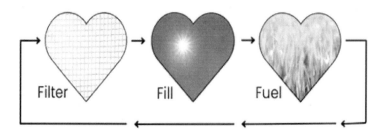

Pillar 1.) Remove Toxins (Filter)

Imagine if our bodies ceased to filter toxins – this would lead to kidney failure and eventual system shutdown. Similarly, in leadership, we often overlook toxins and allow them to accumulate in the nooks and crannies of our beings and our organizations. FullHearted Leadership begins by acknowledging and diagnosing these toxins and barriers, including the resulting gaps they create.

Pillar 2.) Deliver Oxygen (Fill)

Oxygen is synonymous with life and energizes the body. As leaders, we risk cutting off our own "oxygen supply" when we lead by trying to fit in, gain approval, or rotely imitate others. If we are simply checking boxes to achieve metrics, playing solo in a hierarchical system, or operating in a series of transactional exchanges, we might be left gasping for air as if on a high-altitude mountain climb.

In FullHearted Leadership, we amp up our life force energy when connected to and expressing that which differentiates us. The unique intersection of our innate attributes, signature talents, entelechy, superpowers, essence, experience, and expertise equips us to make the contributions only we can make.

From this filled-up state, we can provide "breathing room" for others and for our ideas, businesses, and communities to take flight.

Pillar 3.) Deliver Nourishment (Fuel)

The variety, quality, and quantity of nourishment determine the efficiency and functioning of the body. There is a vast continuum between starving, getting by, thriving, and ultimate peak function.

Just like limited nutrition can lead to dysfunction, deficiencies, and disease in the body, a leadership style that relies on limited facets can lead to diminished functionality, detrimental consequences, and loss of vitality. An over-emphasis on profits over well-being, assertiveness over empathy, short-term gain over sustainability, individual reward over the community, and any number of other dichotomies can lead to a reduced "quality of life."

In FullHearted Leadership, optimum nourishment provides a solid foundation to meet the complexities of today's world. Nourishment originates from the tenets of love, empathy, and excellence, with a deep understanding of the human condition and the interconnectedness of all things. It's about leading through who we are being. It's about what we do when no one else is watching.

Ongoing Improvements

The three pillars of FullHearted Leadership mirror the vital functions of the heart: removing toxins, delivering oxygen, and providing nourishment. Ignoring any of the pillars can result in dire consequences and diminished performance. Regularly cycling through these three pillars of FullHearted Leadership ensures ongoing improvements, optimum functioning, and unlocking the fullest potential and highest contribution in ourselves, our teams, our organizations, our communities, and our world.

FullHearted Leadership Manifesto – The Philosophy

"In a full heart there is room for everything, and in an empty heart there is room for nothing."

Antonio Porcia (Poet)

- FullHearted Leadership is a leadership style and philosophy that centers on embracing the human condition in its entirety.
- FullHearted Leadership is built upon the belief that a full heart can hold all that has been, all that is, and all that is yet to be.
- FullHearted Leadership is ever-evolving.
- FullHearted Leadership is being that which we desire to create.
- FullHearted Leadership cradles paradox.
- FullHearted Leadership believes FullHearted individuals catalyze FullHearted collectives, and FullHearted collectives catalyze FullHearted individuals.
- FullHearted Leadership infuses understanding, breathing room, and nourishment to ignite the brightest and highest outcomes.
- FullHearted Leadership recognizes the mystery of the unknown, the innate wisdom of the body, and the unlimited potential of the human spirit.
- FullHearted Leadership stands as a beacon for unity, wholeness, and authentic connection.

A Call to FullHearted Leadership

You are the most important person you will ever lead.

I invite you to embark on a journey of FullHearted Leadership. It will be the most profound expedition of your life—the journey inward. The degree to which your heart is full is the degree to which you have to extend outside yourself and bring your visions to fruition.

One of the paradoxes of FullHearted Leadership is you do not become yourself by yourself; you become yourself in reflection and relationship to others, the world around you, and life itself. Yet it is all up to you – no one can take the walk for you.

In the realm of FullHearted Leadership, you are be stowed the capacity and courage to embrace yourself and the world with an open and full heart. A heart that can hold and disrupt what has been while unlocking and rewriting what is yet to be.

When you lead yourself into FullHearted Leadership, you become a FullHearted Leader wherever you are - in your family, in your business, in your community, and in a world waiting to be transformed - one full heart at a time.

FullHearted Leadership begins with you. Your heart is calling. What are you waiting for?

Author Bio

Bonnie Lynn

Bonnie Lynn is a visionary trailblazer with over 25 years of experience growing a specialty commercial construction business from inception to $8 million in annual revenues.

Her pioneering spirit and business acumen have been featured in notable publications such as Finance & Commerce and Minnesota Business, alongside accolades including Pioneer of the Year by NAWBO and Expanding Business of the Year by Women Venture.

With a robust academic background highlighted by a B.A. in Mathematics, Bonnie is also an alumnus of SBA Emerging Leaders, Economic Gardening, Women Venture Scale Up, and the Entre Trilogy Leadership Experience.

Her influence extends through her Board of Directors roles, including the *Association of Women Contractors* and the *St. Paul Area Chamber*; and as a founding member of the *Institute for Women-Centered Coaching, Training & Leadership.*

Bonnie's fusion of keen business understanding, heart-focused intelligence and innate knack for revealing camouflaged gaps has evolved a transformative leadership approach. Her firm, Bonify Now, designed the innovative FullHearted Leadership Framework along with customized Coaching Services to cultivate future leaders who dismantle barriers and unlock potential stifled in traditional systems.

- LiveGood@BonifyNow.com
- BonifyNow.com

This is dedicated to my parents Robert and Dorothy

Tillman; I am amazed at the impact they had on me

finding my voice. They taught me life is more than an

abundance of things but rather life's experiences-all

of them.

The Courage to Walk Away:

My Journey to Entrepreneurship

Liz Luckette

The decision to abandon the predictable routine of a conventional 9-5 job and venture into the unknown was undoubtedly a daunting endeavor. Stepping away from the security of a stable professional environment, complete with its established routines, defined roles, and consistent income, was not for the faint-hearted. It was a bold move that brought forth a multitude of questions and uncertainties. Did I make the correct choice? What lies ahead for me? Amid these doubts and anxieties, a familiar voice of wisdom emerged, cutting through the noise and illuminating my path. It was my father, imparting his lifetime of experience. I vividly recall his profound words of wisdom: "Liz, by the time you think you have life all figured out, it's just about over." His insightful perspective served as a wake-up call, bringing a sense of peace intertwined with the fear and excitement of venturing into uncharted territory.

I began to realize that my personal aspirations did not align with the monotony of a traditional 9-5 job. The relentless demands of the competitive corporate world had taken a toll on me. Balancing multiple projects, managing performance metrics, budgeting, and overseeing employees had drained my energy. Dealing with HR issues, resolving customer complaints, meeting sales targets, and navigating office politics had become an overwhelming source of stress. The ceaseless pursuit of corporate objectives, maintaining a facade of workplace camaraderie, advocating for diversity, and engaging in cutthroat competition to advance up the corporate ladder had all contributed to an oppressive environment.

I yearned for liberation from this never-ending cycle, and it was my father's words, spoken shortly before his untimely passing, that sparked a desire for change within me. My father was an exemplar of authenticity and integrity, a man who placed great value on honesty and the power of genuine human connections. He firmly believed in placing faith in a higher power above all else. He lived his life with passion, cherishing each moment as if it were his last. His greatest joys were found in simple pleasures: fishing, hunting, cooking, and nurturing his family.

Despite his imperfections, his authenticity permeated every aspect of his existence. He imparted countless life lessons, but his most profound wisdom lay in his philosophy of facing death with dignity and grace. His grounding presence prepared me for life's uncertainties, and his words—" By time you think you have life all figured out, it's over"— instilled in me a fresh perspective on life. Armed with this newfound revelation, I took the courageous step of walking away from the confines of the corporate world, determined to forge my own path. Embarking on a journey to shape my own destiny, I set out to create a platform that would enable me to pursue my dreams. As I continue to mold a life filled with purpose and fulfillment, one that aligns with my true aspirations, the echoes of my father's wisdom and unwavering support serve as the guiding compass on my journey.

When my father was initially diagnosed with cancer, I made the decision to leave one corporate job for another, seeking stability and security. When he fought and triumphed over the illness, I returned to the familiar corporate environment. But when his health declined again, I realized that I was right back at square one.

After the passing of my father, I found myself caught in the all-too-familiar cycle of the corporate world: a mere three days of bereavement leave. I was expected to process a lifetime of cherished memories in such a painfully inadequate amount of time. But as is often the case in the corporate landscape, my essential role compelled me to answer phone calls. These calls would start with seemingly casual phrases like "we were thinking" or "what about..." and inevitably lead to the crushing statement: "Unfortunately, we won't be able to pay you if you need more time." It became abundantly clear that my personal well-being was of little importance compared to their rigid terms and conditions, leaving me consumed by frustration and a sense of being undervalued.

Upon my return to work, the overwhelming sensation of not belonging persisted. In a desperate attempt to find solace, I applied for another position within the company, hoping for a fresh start. However, my hopes were dashed as I faced rejection. It was in that moment of disappointment that I came to a profound realization: I could no longer endure this disheartening situation. The lack of empathy and support from my corporate environment had taken its toll, and I knew it was time to take control of my own destiny.

I found myself at a crossroads in life. It was a profound moment that made me realize how fleeting our time on this earth truly is. I began to question the path I had been on, dedicating so much of myself to fulfilling someone else's dreams. The dissatisfaction and frustration I felt in my job grew stronger every day, especially when faced with the same monotonous tasks and demands of creating sales campaigns. It became unbearable. Thankfully, my husband saw the toll it was taking on me and offered a simple solution: "If you're unhappy, leave." And so, I did. He assured me that he would support me, urging me to pursue my own dreams and find true fulfillment.

This idea of quitting my job had been lingering in the back of my mind for years, but fear and comfort held me back. I had a stable job with a steady paycheck, a predictable routine, and a sense of security. Leaving all of that behind to start my own business meant stepping into the unknown. It meant giving up the reassurance of knowing what each day would bring. Despite growing tired of the responsibilities that came with corporate America, there were undeniable perks like paid vacations, sick leave, a dedicated office space, and readily available equipment. I had everything I needed at my fingertips. However, if I decided to walk away, it would mark a complete shift in my mindset. I would have to embrace a growth mindset, open to learning, adapting, and taking risks.

I decided I wanted to build my own platform, create my own destiny, and live out my dreams. With my husband's support and wanting to ensure that I would live my life on purpose and not wait until it was just about over, I made the decision to leave.

The Plan

I started by strategically paying off all our credit card debts. This was a crucial step, as I understood that starting my own business would be challenging, and I didn't want to burden my husband with excessive financial pressure. I carefully assessed our credit scores and diligently took steps to improve them. Implementing a well-thought-out spending plan enabled us to stick to a budget while simultaneously chipping away at our debts. It was essential for us to be in a financially stable position while my new business took off.

In addition, I sought guidance from other successful women who had taken the leap and left their jobs to pursue their entrepreneurial dreams. I reached out to them, thirsting for knowledge and insights. I listened attentively, filling pages upon pages with valuable advice and experiences. Their stories varied, with some recommending that they continue working until their side businesses matched their 9-5 incomes, while others insisted on building a solid client base before making the leap. There were even those who initially left but quickly returned to the comforting embrace of corporate America when confronted with the challenges of running a small business.

The Business

Embarking on the journey of starting a business requires a certain level of courage and resilience. Unlike in a traditional work environment, where everything is conveniently provided for you, as an entrepreneur or small business owner, the weight of responsibility falls squarely on your shoulders. It is natural to question whether you have what it takes to handle it all. But let me assure you, you are more than capable of shouldering this burden.

There were moments when doubt crept in, making me question if I could do this. Did I feel I could shoulder this new venture-Absolutely! Were there moments when my shoulders were not broad enough-Absolutely! Yet, it was precisely in those moments that I realized something profound: it is possible to experience conflicting emotions simultaneously. You can be both exhilarated and apprehensive, cautious and audacious, prepared and uncertain. These contradictory feelings coexist within you, propelling you forward amidst the chaos.

And here is the beauty of it all — the chaos is uniquely yours. The business you are building is a manifestation of your vision, passion, and drive. With every challenge you face and overcome, you will develop an unbreakable bond with your venture. That sense of ownership and belonging is truly remarkable.

Remember, those emotions you are experiencing are not only normal but also essential. They are the indicators of growth and progress. So, embrace the duality of your feelings, stand tall in the face of uncertainty, and let these contrasting emotions propel you toward the extraordinary success that awaits you.

Starting a business requires courage and determination. In the corporate world, everything is readily available to you — computers, phones, desks, and buildings. But starting your own business can feel overwhelming. You may have a great product or idea, but where do you even begin?

For me, it all started with the question, "Why?" Why was I doing this? What was my motivation behind starting a business? It wasn't just about having the best product or overcoming challenges to become successful. I had to dig deeper and understand what was truly driving me to take this leap. It wasn't about money or wealth; it was about finding my why.

Ariel Belgrave Harris discussed this topic on a podcast titled "Why Do You Want to Start a Business? Make Sure You are Doing It for The Right Reason." She emphasized the importance of not just running away from something (like corporate America) but running towards something meaningful. Without a strong why, it's difficult to handle the stresses that come with being a business owner. You need to know your true motivation to stay committed and overcome obstacles.

I also came across a TED Talk by Simon Sinek called "How Great Leaders Inspire Action." It resonated with me and helped me put into words what I couldn't articulate myself. Sinek explained that your motivation goes beyond tangible factors like market success or key indicators. Your why is intangible and stems from your beliefs. It's not about what you do but why you do it. Simon Sinek: "People do not buy what you do; they buy why you do it, and what you do simply proves what you believe. In fact, people will do the things that prove what they believe."

Lisa Nichols, a 7-time New York Times bestselling author, emphasized the importance of aligning with your why in her video "Find your WHY. Align with your WHY. Be confident in your WHY." Even when you may be uncertain about what, people will be drawn to your why if it is solid and authentic.

In the world of business, it's not just about the tangible aspects but also the intangibles. To realize your vision, you must focus on what you can't see.

Now, let's talk about dreams. We all have those dreams that consume our thoughts, converging the line between reality and imagination. It's where reality and destiny collide. But how do we make sure our dreams become a reality? The first step is to determine if your dream is truly yours. In her book "The Blueprint to Manifesting Your Dreams: Crystallize Your Vision," Mariko Bennett emphasizes the significance of clarifying your dream before pursuing it.

Turning an intangible dream into something tangible starts with writing it down. You need to materialize your vision by transforming it from imagination to reality. This takes courage and skill, but it all begins with the simple act of putting pen to paper.

As an entrepreneur, you possess visionary qualities. But it's important to transition from the realm of dreams to the actualization of your dream. In the dream world, you can fly, walk through walls, and leap over buildings in a single bound- You can be the Superhero. In the real world, you will face obstacles, and when you come to a wall, you quickly realize that you can't walk through it. You need to plan and strategize to overcome them. Henry Ford and George Washington Carver are great examples of visionaries who brought their dreams to life.

Envisioning, strategizing, and implementing are key steps in the VSI model - Vision, Strategy, and Implementation. Once you have determined your why and crystallized your dream, it's time to focus on what you want to achieve and the problem you want to solve.

Vision is like seeing clearly for the first time. Just like how my eye surgery allowed me to see the world with enhanced clarity, having a vision for your business brings everything into focus. As Helen Keller once said, "The only thing worse than being blind is having sight but no vision."

Your idea or thought takes you from your present and carries you into the future. Just like Ford and Carver, who had revolutionary visions, you must take what's in your head and help others see it and believe in it.

Strategy sets your vision in motion. It involves not just focusing on success but anticipating challenges and finding solutions. It's like playing chess, where each piece moves according to its unique ability. To achieve your goals, you need a clear roadmap, guiding principles, and a prioritization plan .

Implementation is the crucial step in implementing your plan. You can dream, talk, and think about it all day, but at some point, you must take that leap and do it. Start by taking small actions, testing your idea on trusted individuals, and seeking feedback. Research is also vital to understanding your industry, competitors, and trends.

The VSI model is a powerful tool for turning your vision into reality, but it requires dedication and hard work.

I did it. I took the leap, and I want to help others step out into unchartered territory. For those who are out there and facing the wall and feel stuck, I want to help them get unstuck.

I am here to help small business owners like you realize their dreams. Connect with me on social media, and together, we can find your vision, find your voice, and get you on the path to success.

Let's get out of the clouds and turn our dreams into thriving businesses. You have within you the courage to walk away from the mundane and walk out your dreams- you just have to take the first step.

Author Bio

Liz Luckett

Liz Luckett is the CEO of Xpressly Speaking Inc. and proud army veteran of the United States of America. She received her Business Administration and Bachelor of Science in Human Services degrees from Cardinal Stritch University.

She is a wife and mother of three who spent 25 years in the Banking and Finance Industry. She took that financial acumen as well as her passion for public speaking to help create Xpressly Speaking Inc.

X-pressly Speaking is a company that is committed to building and creating platforms to help clients, organizations, and mutual minds advance their personal goal and mission by finding their voice. As a transformational coach, Liz executes expertise in public speaking, keynote addressing, one on one coaching, small group writing and financial wellness workshops. As an author she passionately navigates through the realities of life to extract a poetic masterpiece. She understands that the power of words combined with the passion of purpose will ignite the change needed in the community she serves.

Liz, along with two other women recently wrote and received a grant on a behalf of a nonprofit in her area for 2.7 million to provide technical assistance to entrepreneurs in all stages of business. The program seeks to help small business get beyond the product to understanding the "business of business."

- linkedin.com/in/elizabeth-luckett-58693953/
- xpresslyspeaking.com/

I dedicate my chapter to my daughter, Lauren. I want her to know that "who you are matters most," and to always speak up for yourself. Money can be your friend, learn to dance with it! Lauren, you are my inspiration! Love you, Mom

You've come
a long way, baby!

Linda Lingo

"What we know matters, but who we are matters more."
- Brene Brown

I love numbers! Always have, always will. They don't talk back or argue. They're consistent and always add up! So, I decided to be a CPA, Certified Public Accountant. I'm also very responsible, being the oldest of five kids growing up on a farm. I thought being a CPA would give me authority and respect in a corporate world. Being the overachiever I am, I studied diligently for months and passed all four parts of the CPA the first time I took the exam. At that time only 20% of the people taking the exam passed all four parts on their first try.

I also had my sights set on a national firm, so I interviewed and was hired by Ernst & Whinney who later merged and became Ernst & Young. I was the only woman hired that year in an office of 80 people. There was one female partner out of five, which was high for the 80's.

Being a CPA is not glamorous, and took a lot of dedication, long hours, and constant maneuvering as to how a woman fit into a man's world.

Working 80 hours a week was the norm in order to get promoted. So I did it, and I got promoted from staff accountant to senior staff accountant to manager and then senior manager. Next step was partner. After eight years of long days and a grueling schedule, I was a senior manager. I was almost to the top! I had delayed having a family for this very reason. I wanted to be a partner. I was tenacious!

BUT life doesn't always turn out as planned, and I became pregnant. Actually I caved into the pressure from my husband. He wanted a family. I wanted a career.

Due to the perceptions that mothers didn't make good partners because they couldn't stay focused on work and had too many distractions with their personal life, I waited until I was six months pregnant to tell the manager partner.

I will never forget his reaction. He didn't ask how I was feeling. He said, "How could you do this to me?" What? I was his top performing Senior Manager CPA, and now I was "letting him down" because I was pregnant!

I went over my plan for how my clients would be served while I took a quick six weeks leave to have the baby and get back to work. But I was never considered in the same professional light once I had my baby.

I felt like I'd done everything 'right' by the corporate standards, but once I was pregnant, I became 'less than.' Men didn't have to worry about breastfeeding or pumping while at work. Men didn't have to worry about day care for a newborn. Men just didn't get it!! Yet women were expected to be 'SuperWoman' and 'balance' everything.

In the 80s, you couldn't talk about your personal or home life at the office. You were there to work and make money for the company. Leadership was not concerned about work/life balance. That was not even discussed!

However, younger women staff accountants looked up to me as a role model, so I had very vulnerable discussions with them. We talked about the hours and demands of the job, and ,or even if, you could balance those with having a family.

After my brief maternity leave, I returned to work and soon realized I wouldn't be advancing to partner, so I started looking around for another way to use my CPA experience.

At the same time, I was trying to find reliable babysitters for my little one. It was so hard to leave him every day. Unfortunately, I gave up on breast feeding him at an early age as a result of my crazy schedule.

In order to "not rock the boat" at the CPA firm, I took sick days to interview for new jobs. The craziest one was flying a red eye flight from California to New York City for the interview with the subsidiary of a Fortune 500 company for controller. It was a great interview, but I found myself having to "sell" over and over that I could balance being a mother and a corporate controller. The hours, the travel, the work. Was I up to it???

What bullshit! I'm sure they didn't ask the male interviewees if they could handle home and work and travel! I had the credentials and was confident I could do the job, and I reinforced that in my interview.

Salary negotiation was interesting, too. I knew what the job was worth and yet was offered 20% less! I had to negotiate to get another 10%, so I got paid 90% of what men doing the same job got paid. Pay disparity was a real thing in the 90s and still is!!

I was the only woman corporate controller for this company, so meetings were full of testosterone! I'd never heard the f**k word so many times in one sentence as I did then! But I didn't let that get to me. I was determined to show them that a woman is as good, if not better, than a man as a corporate controller. I was persistent, tenacious and excelled!

I was asked to participate in a management training program which required traveling from California to NYC every other week for two years. Of course I took it! I wanted to advance in corporate America, and I wanted to show women in the company they could excel and be promoted as well.

I was trying to keep "all the balls in the air" (balance home and work). My husband liked the income but wouldn't help with childcare or household chores. So I hired a live-in nanny. She was a godsend. But my controlling narcissistic husband didn't like the food she cooked or the fact that she was teaching our 18 month old son Spanish. There was constant tension.

I found out the hard way it's critical to be on the same page with your spouse when it comes to having a family and the expectations of each partner. Because of the stress of the job and travel and tension at home, I suffered two miscarriages over an eight year period .

Guys don't have miscarriages, and it's not something women talk about very much. But it affects women of all ages. I worked in an environment of primarily men, so taking time off to grieve after my miscarriages was not done. That's one regret I have to this day, not taking time to feel the emotions of losing my babies. But, I wanted to be stellar, responsible, earn my five-star rating as a corporate controller, and I did.

Being a lone female in a male corporate world was difficult, demanding, and crazy! Why was I doing this? To earn my five-star rating– prove my worth through my achievements? Probably. However, suffering from burnout, stress, adrenal fatigue, I left this position after almost ten years.

Regaining my sense of stability, and allowing my stress level to come back to "normal" took six months. I had no idea the adrenaline I was running on until I was out of the workplace.

Upon realizing how burned out I was from my corporate career, I decided it was time to take a break and be a stay-at-home mom for my son, and I did! I loved volunteering in his classroom and helping him with his homework.

At age 44 I became pregnant with my daughter! Wow, what a surprise!! My pregnancy freaked out my female OBGYN, but I felt great. I ate healthy and exercised and loved being pregnant. I chose to have her via natural birth, and she came quickly! We bonded immediately and I nursed her for 18 months! We were inseparable. I was going to do everything "right" with this child.

Well, every child is different, and truth be told, there is no "right" way. As a mother, I think you figure it out as you go along. I truly believe it takes a tribe to raise children, so I relied on my best friends, as I had no family close by.

Since leaving my corporate job, I'd rolled my 401(k) into an IRA with a local financial advisor. It was time for my "annual review" so I went in prepared with my statement and list of questions. He was a typical white male financial advisor, sitting behind his very large, walnut wood desk in his big office chair.

After getting the pleasantries out of the way, I started asking my questions about my investments. He couldn't answer my first question, so I figured I must be asking it the wrong way. (Why do we women second guess ourselves?) So I rephrased the question, and he still couldn't answer it! He was getting agitated with me! The third time I tried rephrasing the question, he leaned over his desk, put his hand on top of my hand and said, "Honey, if you do what I say, you'll be just fine." WTF??????

I pulled my hand away, gathered up my papers, stood up, shook hands, said thank you (really? thank you for trying to intimidate me and be condescending) and walked out of his office. I thought to myself, I will never be back in this office, and I can do this job better than he can. I also didn't want another woman to have this horrible condescending, intimidating experience with their financial advisor. So I went home and googled how to become a financial advisor.

After four months of intense study and exams, I was a licensed financial advisor and had landed a job with a large advisory firm.

Unlike the men who usually received an office with existing clients, I was given an office with ZERO clients, so I had to develop my own relationships and bring in my own clients. My relationships ran deep. I could tell you where they lived, what they did for a living, how many kids they had, and the name of their dog. It was about more than their investments, it was about their lives! I think this is part of what differentiates men from women financial advisors. Men tend to be transactional while women are relational.

When my clients came into my office, I seated them at a small round table and sat next to the woman so she knew I was on her side. I was not intimidating, although I was very confident in what I did and the advice I gave. I wanted to be a woman's advocate for their money, investments, goals, and life plan.

I loved being a financial advisor, but also realized that women want more education before they make an investment decision. They want to know why this investment is good for them. Women typically make better investors when they understand what they're investing in and how it aligns with their financial goals. As a result, they will stay invested longer and not realize short term losses.

After serving my clients for almost ten years, I pivoted from a financial advisor to a financial life coach. I listened to my own intuition. I wanted to guide and educate women in their finances, especially as they were experiencing a life transition.

But this was the first time I was on my own! No regular paycheck. Once again I was building my business from ground zero. So I did it the way I knew how, personal networking. I love connecting with women, it's actually one of my super powers. I'm very intuitive and can sense when they are struggling, especially with money. And so I built my financial life coaching business one client at a time.

I found that when midlife women experience a transition like divorce, death of a spouse, empty nester, or career change, finances become a priority for them. When they turn 50, it's "OMG, I've got to kick my retirement plan into high gear!" They're motivated to learn and make necessary changes to accomplish their goals.

Because I've lived many of these life transitions, I guide women based on my life experiences, and education. I can relate to their emotions and feelings of being scared and anxious. I inspire women to transform from surviving these experiences to thriving afterwards. I use unconventional methods in my coaching because money is such an important aspect of our daily lives.

Women who work with me have seen dramatic shifts in their mindset and eliminated money blocks, thus opening them up to expansive shifts in their energy and income opportunities. They transform from fear and anxiety about their money to gratitude and abundance.

They learn to dance with money, make money their best friend, and have confidence with their finances. Women learn to make their own intentional money spending and saving plan that is in alignment with their values which gives them great joy.

I work with the money issues that will save my clients thousands of dollars, and not stress over the $4 latte. We address what will have huge, lasting impacts on their lives and their finances.

Looking back on my journey, I am thankful I took advantage of a variety of career opportunities. Each position gave me experience in a new field. Yes, they all used my MBA in Finance and CPA certificate and each position broadened my base of knowledge.

In each of my corporate positions, women were definitely in the minority. I mentored many young women and sought mentors for myself. I strongly encourage women to seek out mentors and be mentors to help women coming up behind them. It's also important to realize that not everyone will like you, but you do want their respect.

To gain respect, I believe you have to be technically proficient and also have good communication skills. Learning the art of negotiation early in your career is vital to get paid on par with men.

I also believe you have to follow your intuition. If a job isn't aligning with your values and goals, then change! Don't stay stuck! It will drain the life out of you.

If I have one piece of advice for younger women, it's that I believe it's important to speak up and let your voice be heard, because "who you are matters most."

Author Bio

Linda Lingo

Linda's passion is guiding and helping women to embrace their financial power so they can change the world. Linda does this by helping women make money their best friend.

Linda Lingo is an authority on women building wealth. Her successful 35 year career in corporate America and her 10 years as a Financial Advisor has given her practical experience, radical knowledge and a deep understanding of the best ways to manage money for the modern day woman.

Women work with Linda to discover how to become a master at their finances, build their wealth and make an even bigger impact in the world. Linda's mission is to empower women with smart strategies for a successful, stress-free approach to money. Through inspiration and education, Linda guides women into clarity and confidence in their finances so they can live the life they desire.

Linda has her MBA in Finance and has served as a Corporate Controller in a Fortune 500 company and CPA with Ernst & Young CPAs.

A few of the podcasts Linda has been featured on include:
Ellen Rogin and Horse's Mouth
Kim O'Hara, "You should write a book about that"
Lesa Koski, "Doing Divorce Differently

Linda's story of why she became a Financial Advisor was featured here:
wealthmanagement.com/client-relations/my-life-client-condescending-and-belittling

• linkedin.com/in/lindalingo/

"I dedicate my chapter to my daughter, Kaleigh Kerr,

the strongest WARRIOR woman I know. Your resilience

& courage is inspiring."

Warrior Women in Leadership

Catherine Kerr

"Courage, above all things, is the first quality of a warrior."
— Carl von Clausewitz, *General & Military Strategist*

The warrior mindset has been around for hundreds, if not thousands, of years. It has nothing to do with aggression or violence but everything to do with developing the mental fortitude and skills to overcome life's challenges with grit and tenacity.

Warriors are Strategic, Focused, Intentional, Resilient, Genuine and **COURAGEOUS**.

Carl von Clausewitz was a Prussian Military General, a brilliant strategist, and theorist. He wrote "On War," a book about military strategy that is still studied today. Carl von Clausewitz said that courage is the FIRST quality of a warrior, and I believe it is the main characteristic we need to develop as women in leadership to have the greatest impact.

Like most, if not all, women, I was not taught courage, I learned it the hard way: through being knocked down time and again, picking myself up, and moving forward without excuses or blaming other people or circumstances. I have earned the right to call myself a Warrior Leader and made it my life's mission to help other women elevate *their* leadership by developing the mindset and behaviours of a warrior.

In this chapter, I will share a part of my personal warrior journey and some tangible tactics you can use to step into your power and become the strong, capable, impactful leader you were born to be.

I worked as a contract facilitator for other sales training companies for over two decades before going out on my own and forming my company, "Kerrageous." Why did it take me so long? In hindsight, I allowed other people to diminish my worth and keep me small. Sound familiar? And, to be honest, and vulnerable with you, I had some old messages in my head telling me that I was "not good enough" that was holding me back from maximizing my full potential.

I am sure you have heard about the "imposter syndrome" many high-performing women feel. Despite our abilities, we believe it's only a matter of time before someone figures out we are unqualified or incompetent and fires us. In my mind, I was one step away from living in a van down by the river, eating cat food. Jeeshhh.

I have had the privilege of facilitating all over the world (Latin America, Asia, the U.K., USA, and Canada), and the number one question female leaders ask me in private is, "How can I become more confident in my leadership abilities?" Over the course of 24 years, I have had C-Suite Leaders confide in me over coffee or a glass of wine (or two) that they feel insecure in their leadership abilities.

One of the greatest challenges that women in leadership face is a lack of self-worth. It takes courage to step into your power and truly own your value. I get it...been there...bought the T-shirt.

When the Pandemic hit and my industry (learning and development) quickly pivoted to virtual, I panicked. I am not a "techy" person; in fact, navigating technology made me very anxious. And even if I had the technical skills, the idea of connecting with people virtually (vs. in person) was not appealing. Then there was the compensation; my fee was reduced dramatically by the companies that were contracting me for my skills. I began asking myself some hard questions:

- What is the value that I am bringing to the table? What is that actual worth in terms of dollars?
- What impact do I want to make, and am I currently making that?
- What would it look like if I were to create a bigger, better, bolder life for myself?
- And most importantly, did I have the COURAGE to bet on myself??

"You Are One Decision Away from a Completely Different Life"
- Mel Robbins, Author of "The 5 Second Rule: Transform Your Life, Work, and Confidence with Everyday Courage"

(BTW, in case you are wondering, I put on my big girl panties and figured out the tech part. I became a vILT (virtual instructor-led trainer) on multiple platforms. Today, I facilitate both virtual and in-person.

The warrior metaphor was born out of a couple of significant life events. Yes, there was some trauma, but I won't get into the details of that. We all struggle, we all have challenges and we all have a story. My painful past is no lesser or greater than yours. What may be different is how we reacted to it.

You see, I have this theory about the difference between a survivor and a warrior. The difference is that the survivor just, well...survives. They just get by. The warrior has the exact same experiences, but she is driven to turn those same challenges into success. The warrior woman doesn't just survive; she thrives.

Boxing came into my life as a way to deal with my mother's cancer. I discovered a boxing class when I was helping to care for my mom in the last few months of her life. Boxing started as a way to deal with stress, but what I gained was so much more. It gave me inner strength and a determination to overcome the challenges yet to come. It gave me the confidence and fearlessness to conquer anything or anyone, including myself. Boxing gave me "grit" and the firm knowledge that no matter what life throws at me, I know how to get up and keep moving forward.

"Kerrageous" was formed out of a strong desire to step into my own power and to empower other women to step into theirs by adopting the mindset and behaviour of a warrior so they could become more courageous and strategic.

Courageous Communication Skills:

Warrior leaders D.R.I.V.E.™ strategic conversations by using courageous communication skills. This is my core model, and all my programs have this as a foundation. D.R.I.V.E.™ stands for:

DISARM OBJECTIONS: 4 Key Tactics
REFLECT/RESTATE EXPERIENCES: Demonstrating deep Empathy
INSIGHTS: Share insights that add value
VERIFY PRIORITY NEED: Assess needs and verify the priority need
ENERGY: Energy rituals to sustain high performance

I explore this acronym in depth in my "Warrior Leadership" workshops. This model contains specific, targeted communication skills, one of which is the ability to ask courageous questions.

One of the most effective ways to immediately dial up the impact of your communication is to ask better questions.

A Courageous Question is:
- Open Ended
- Invites Reflection
- Starts with an **Action Verb**: e.g., Describe, Explain, Tell, Share, Predict, Outline, Clarify, Compare, Define, Summarize, Assess, Identify

3 C's:
- Challenges Current Thinking
- Creates Constructive Tension &/or
- Causes Insight and Understanding

Here are some examples of Courageous Questions:
- "**Identify** what you need to be doing differently or better in your role as X."
- "**Share** with me the greatest challenge you are currently struggling with in your role."
- "**Describe** how I can best support you."
- "**Assess** this situation from the customer's point of view."
- "**Outline** your plan to improve your product knowledge by the end of this year."
- "**Summarize** the value that you feel you bring to our customers."
- "**Describe** what you believe would be a better way."
- "**Describe** the steps/process you take when dealing with conflict or disagreement with a colleague."
- "**Outline** your plan to achieve our growth targets."
- "**Tell** me what I need to be doing differently or better as your leader to add greater value."
- "**Define** the ideal solution for this problem."
- "**Compare** your results from last quarter to this quarter."

You may have noticed that these questions seem more like statements. That is by design. There is nowhere to hide with a courageous question! Again, these are to be used strategically (not every question can or should be courageous; that would be exhausting!).

The ultimate value of these questions is that they drive a deeper, more meaningful conversation.

So why wouldn't we ask these kinds of questions? Because we either 1) are making assumptions (and therefore don't ask questions because we think we know the answer), or 2) we lack the courage.

"We make all sorts of assumptions because we don't have the COURAGE to ask questions."

- Miguel Angel Ruiz, *The Four Agreements*

Here's a suggestion: Practice courageous questions on random strangers...the barista at Starbucks, your Uber driver, etc. What have you got to lose? Watch how people react! You will be surprised by how eager people are to engage. My theory behind this is that people are hungry for connection.

Tip: Be Intensely Curious!

Curiosity is a driver to ask better questions. In fact, there is a direct correlation between courage and curiosity! The more courageous you are, the more curious you become. One way to dial up your curiosity is to ask questions that you genuinely do not know the answer to.

Courageously Communicating Change:

Courageously communicating change is another essential way that women in leadership can help transform their companies and step into warrior leadership.

Given that women tend to have high empathy and genuinely care about their teams and colleagues, having a *strategy* for navigating these conversations is extremely helpful for creating sustained change over time.

On the flip side, women tend to be conflict-averse (I am, of course, generalizing) and therefore avoid or diminish the intensity of these types of conversations. I believe that having a process for navigating these conversations takes away some of that fear.

I have an MEd with a specialization in Counselling Psychology, and therefore, I like to integrate/leverage psychology into my training sessions. One of the models that you may or may not be familiar with is the Behavioural Change Model. In a nutshell, this model tells us that **AWARENESS** precedes changes.

However, awareness alone is not enough to make someone change. The person also has to be **WILLING**.

Awareness plus willingness are still not enough. People need to also understand and really believe in the **BENEFIT** of change.

Saying that awareness + willingness + benefit is *still* not enough to create *sustained* changes in behaviour.

In order to create sustained changes in behaviour, there also needs to be **SUPPORT** and/or **COACHING** put in place for when they will struggle.

CREATING BEHAVIOURAL CHANGE:

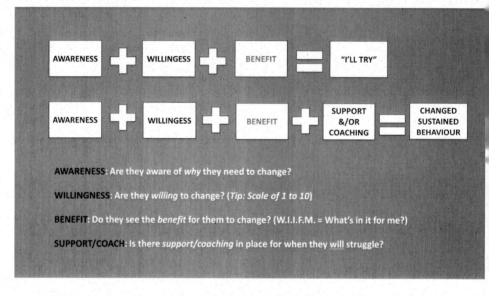

AWARENESS: Are they aware of *why* they need to change?

WILLINGNESS: Are they *willing* to change? (*Tip: Scale of 1 to 10*)

BENEFIT: Do they see the *benefit* for them to change? (W.I.I.F.M. = What's in it for me?)

SUPPORT/COACH: Is there *support/coaching* in place for when they <u>will</u> struggle?

COURAGEOUSLY COMMUNICATING CHANGE PROCESS:

CREATE AWARENESS: Are they aware of why we need to change? Create Awareness by:
- Asking Courageous Questions
- Be Curious & Compassionate (Be kind to yourself and others)

ASSESS LEVEL OF WILLINGNESS: Are they willing to change? Drill down!
- *"On a scale of 1 -10, where 1 = 'I am completely not willing to change,' and 10 = 'I am 100% willing to change,' where are you?"*
- *"Why that number?"*
- *"What needs to happen to move you closer to an 8?"*

DETERMINE THE BENEFIT: Do they see the benefit for them to change?

- Understanding **W.I.F.M.** (What is in it for me?) creates greater buy-in.
- Knowing the benefit will increase their ability to remain resilient and stay the course as we navigate change.

PROVIDE ON-GOING SUPPORT/COACHING: Is there support in place for when they will struggle?
- Normalize the struggle: "Change is hard; we all struggle, and setbacks are to be expected."
- Support is KEY to ensuring sustained, changed behaviour.
- Assess the level of support/coaching required for each unique individual.

"We can choose courage or we can choose comfort, but we can't have both. Not at the same time."

– Brené Brown, Author

If we want to expand our capacity, whether that is our mental, emotional, or physical capacity, we have to get out of our comfort zone. We must step out with courage, take a risk, and embrace discomfort. We *can not* grow or change without discomfort. IF you choose to embrace the path of a warrior, you will be uncomfortable...A LOT.

Warrior Leadership begins with the development of resiliency or "grit." Part of resiliency is the ability to handle the pressure/stress of communicating change. It's okay to feel fearful. Courage is not the absence of fear but acting despite it.

As a final thought, I feel compelled to add that women in leadership need to TRUST themselves more. You have earned the right to be here.

In my "Warrior Leadership" workshops, I ask leaders to write a Personal Performance Statement. If you would like to give this a shot, use the formula "I must ...." "So that ...."

What must you DO to be a more courageous leader? Suggestion: pick some of the behaviours outlined in this chapter!

And what is the BENEFIT? I hope that you see benefits in becoming a more courageous leader, first and foremost for yourself and secondly for your direct reports/company/clients. Hopefully, you see the benefits for your personal life as well, not just for your professional career.

In moments of doubt, remember that you are braver than you know and stronger than you feel... you are a goddamn WARRIOR!

WHAT'S NEXT?

When you attend a "Warrior Leadership" workshop, you can expect to learn and actively practice:

- The Warrior Mindset
- Courageous Communication Skills
- How to D.R.I.V.E.™ Strategic Conversations
- Courageous Feedback
- How to Courageously Communicate Change

The combination of courage and strategy will allow you to take your leadership skills to the next level and have a greater impact.

If you would like to join my "tribe" of high-performing "Warrior Women," look for me on LinkedIn and let me know how I can best support you and your team! Let's work together to elevate women in leadership!

From one warrior to another, I wish you well on your Warrior Leadership journey.

Author Bio

Catherine Kerr

Catherine Kerr is the CEO and Founder of Kerrageous. As a warrior coach, keynote speaker and global facilitator, she empowers leaders and their teams to up-level their performance and maximize results.

She specializes in working with sales teams and leaders in the financial services industry – asset and wealth management specifically – but her skills/concepts are applicable to any workplace team.

Catherine has over 25 years of experience in sales, consulting and facilitation, prior to which she was a tenacious and successful entrepreneur. She has a background in boxing, theatre, a Master's Degree in Education with a speciality in Counselling Psychology and has coached Olympic Athletes on the power of mindset.

By combining her diverse background with years of research into high performance, Catherine has created a unique and impactful "Warrior Development Plan" that challenges and inspires leaders and their teams to develop the mindset and behaviours of a WARRIOR so they can D.R.I.V.E.™ strategic conversations, add value, radically improve performance, and ultimately drive revenue.

Catherine lives in Toronto, Canada. She enjoys yoga, old movies and travelling the world.

- catherine@kerrageous.ca

This chapter is dedicated to my two amazing kids who have taught me so much and inspire me everyday. Being their mom is my greatest honour and has changed my life in every way possible.

Transforming Our Response to Grief:

The Role of Women Leaders

Suzanne Jabour

Imagine the moment you encounter someone who is experiencing grief and loss from a death, financial crisis, an incident in the news, or some other challenge. You can sense something is wrong. You don't know what to say or do, and you hesitate. You blurt out something and wish you could take it back. Or you say nothing and hope the person will go about their business as they did before. You don't provide support. You hope it will be okay. You wish you could have done something differently.

Now, carry that situation into the workplace. Business and organizational leaders often don't understand they are unintentionally doing harm. It's impacting staff retention and negatively affecting the bottom line. Employees are abandoned and suffering when you could make small yet significant changes to improve their experience and how they show up at work. You can fix it.

In a study released in 2024, Empathy.com looked specifically at grief in the workplace and calculated the annual cost of hidden grief in the US workplace at over $100 billion. We would intervene in any other situation where businesses incur such a high cost. Unfortunately, our collective fear and lack of knowledge about grief mean this very expensive problem remains unaddressed. When employers can find the grief, acknowledge it, and support those experiencing it, they effectively build retention, engagement, and productivity, which boosts the bottom line.

No matter how robust the health and wellness programming is or how supportive the workplace culture is, there is an unrecognized gap in this area that mirrors the gap in our society. We don't know enough about grief to support each other, nor do we know enough about each other to know when we might be experiencing it. When that grief comes to work, we see staff withdrawal and burnout. We see leaves of absence. What is even more absent is a helpful and meaningful response.

Women in leadership can lead the movement to change all of that, impacting the overall wellness of people and organizations.

In September 2020, I was away for the weekend with my daughter and got the middle-of-the-night phone call every parent dreads. The police were calling to notify me that my son, Ben, had died. My world instantly crashed to pieces around me. And yet, I had to keep going. I went to tell my daughter; we called Ben's dad, and somehow packed our things and drove home.

And then we had to figure out how to do all the impossibly hard things that come after the death of a loved one while our hearts and lives were shattered. We had to figure out how to survive.

I knew very early on that to survive, I had to grieve out loud. Most grievers don't make that choice. I had to be honest about how I was feeling and doing. And I had to talk about it. I spoke to anyone who gave me an opening. I learned very quickly that when I was asked, "How are you?" not everyone actually wanted to know how I was doing. Most people really wanted me to say I was fine and allow the conversation to move on, as has become the normal interaction in our culture. As that was impossible, I stopped answering "How are you?" altogether.

I also knew I needed to stay conscious and curious, and that became my mantra. Conscious of all the emotions, denying none. Conscious of what I needed in any given moment and allowing that to be okay. Conscious of small choices I had to make many times a day about how to continue. How to just breathe. Curiosity in the early days was mostly about that. How, when you are sobbing so hard you can only gasp, do you breathe? What tools do I have in my toolbox that I can access? How do you get through the day when every moment is excruciating, and the world you are inhabiting is a post-apocalyptic nightmare? How on earth did grief work? When making a grilled sandwich took forty-five minutes, how was I supposed to go to work?

I knew I didn't know enough about grief to be able to do it. I needed to know if what was happening to me emotionally, physically, and psychologically was normal. My lack of knowledge was now scary. My son had died, the me I knew no longer existed, and I had some kind of sudden onset brain disease because my brain didn't function anymore either. I became a student of grief out of necessity. I needed to understand what was going on with me and if any of it was something I needed to worry about.

I started writing about what I was experiencing as a matter of survival. I needed to get the spin out of my head and share my reality. It was a way to connect with the rest of the world that seemed to be continuing without me. It was also a way to feel connection at a time when I had retreated from a world that appeared not to know or care that there had been a cataclysmic shift in my reality.

As I followed my path of curiosity, I became fascinated with the truth held by most grievers that "grief changes your address book." In the early days, as I engaged with online groups, I kept wondering why people kept saying that. Surely, the people I had relied on before Ben died would continue to be the people I relied on. But no. Over time, it became clear that most people didn't have the ability to show up for a grieving mom, especially one who was grieving out loud.

When I do a survey or ask in a workshop why people were held back from showing up fully for someone in grief, the overwhelming response is "fear." We fear doing the wrong thing. We fear making it worse. We fear doing harm. We get frozen. And then, beyond offering condolences, cards, or flowers, we do nothing. Time passes, and the opportunity passes. It gets more awkward to step forward, and the myth of the grief timeline lets us off the hook as, surely, we think, they are done grieving. The griever's address book changes.

When it comes to grief, we need leaders who will step up into learning, embrace the awkwardness that comes with change, and open the conversations. Whether you are a leader in your community, organization, or business, grievers need you to join the wave of change. I know it might feel scary stepping into a big, messy emotional space that remains taboo, but we need to be courageous and do it anyway. It's become my mission and business to help you do so.

When I talk about grief, I want to be sure you expand the definition to see that grief comes from losses of all kinds, big and small. It comes with change, especially with changes we didn't want or didn't expect, but it can also come with change for the better.

When we acknowledge grief as a healthy response to losses of all kinds, it shifts the conversation. We can quickly see that we are often in some level of grief. We all experience losses, disappointments, uncertainty, and change now more than ever. With our global connectedness, we also experience vicarious grief for things not happening directly to us but happening in our community locally or on the other side of the globe.

To be able to understand what's happening to us and grieve healthfully, we all need basic grief knowledge. While grief is different every time, some common symptoms, experiences, and activators are universal. The more we understand grief, the less scary it is for the griever and those supporting them. Had I known in those early days that brain fog, or grief brain, was a very normal experience, I would not have worried there was something wrong with me. Knowledge gives us comfort.

Here are some common symptoms of grief that it is helpful to know about:
- brain fog, including confusion and memory lapses
- sleeplessness (or sleeping too much)
- issues with food and eating
- tingling in extremities
- muscle pain and fatigue
- digestive upset
- disrupted relationship with time
- disconnection from the "normal" world
- overwhelming emotions

Think back. How many times when you or someone you care about has been experiencing grief have one of those symptoms occurred? How did you respond? Now that you know they are normal, would you respond differently? Understanding that grief brings with it many of those symptoms, to varying degrees, at various times, don't you feel better? I sure did. When I knew that what was happening to me was expected, it meant I didn't need to worry. I could accept it, know the symptoms would pass, and get on with grieving.

In our workplaces, we can offer specific supports to help with the typical symptoms. Brain fog is the symptom that has the most impact in the workplace. We can support people with documentation of steps needed to perform tasks and timelines for deliverables. We can set reminders for meetings and deadlines. We can take extra care of our people in safety-sensitive positions as we know distraction and safety don't go well together. We can have conversations with people from every level in the organization to brainstorm ideas and see what we can offer. The more options, the better, as every griever is different, and their needs change over time.

The other critical thing to understand is the grief timeline. It's simplest to think about four phases as defined by David Kessler: anticipatory grief, acute grief, early grief, and mature grief. While there is no set timeline, and each grief will be different, there is a range of experience that helps supporters understand how long someone might need assistance.

Anticipatory grief comes before the loss. It happens in cases of terminal illness, dementia, and when we know a change is coming – like moving or closing a business. Sometimes, anticipatory grief lessens the grief when the change finally happens, but not always. It can be helpful with closure and lessening regrets. We are given a chance to say and do what we need to have a clearer relationship with the person or experience. With the aging population, many people have responsibilities related to elder care, which impacts their abilities. If this also involves illness, the impact is increased.

Acute grief is from the first days and can continue up to ten months after someone has died or the change has happened. The symptoms are most disruptive and continual in this phase, and grievers need support. Imagine not feeling connected to time, your brain, or the rest of the world and having to go to work and be productive, often with the expectation that you will behave like nothing has happened. The typical bereavement leave in North America is three to five days. Grievers are still trying to make sense of the impossible and are expected to be back at work, participating and productive. It's an impossible task for many and an unreasonable ask for most. Leaders need to step up in this phase to support people to stay as connected and productive as they are able.

Early grief is the first two years. We all understand that the firsts are supposed to be hard. And they are. Often, the seconds are worse. Grievers are moving beyond the acute survival phase and reintegrating further with life. They now clearly see the new reality and have a better ability to navigate symptoms and emotions. The grief activators, both predictable (like significant dates) and unpredictable (like a song on the grocery store muzak), are still strong. In this period, acknowledging the significant dates really helps the griever feel less alone. So often, it feels like the world has gone on as if nothing happened—the fact you remember and reach out makes a difference.

Mature grief is the grief we carry for the rest of our lives. We've integrated our loss and our grief and think of what we've lost with more love than pain. Most days, we are fine, though we may never be our old selves. There are still moments when grief overwhelms us, but they are farther and farther apart.

Why does all this knowledge matter? It matters because our lack of understanding and collective inability to robustly support each other mean that grievers are suffering. We can change that.

When we understand grief better, we can move from fear to compassion and support people experiencing it. We can use our understanding that grief comes from all kinds of loss to find opportunities to practice grief support so that when the big losses happen, we are more confident and able to step up and less likely to do harm.

In our businesses and communities, there are countless opportunities to practice. When we launch a product and it fails. When we have quarterly earnings that are not what we expected. When our offices move, or we reorganize. When something happens in our community that creates collective grief. When customers or clients die. If we shift the conversation to acknowledge the emotions that come with those losses, we open up space to practice. As leaders, we need to lead. No team member can be more vulnerable and honest than the leader.

What if our debrief meeting started with the leader acknowledging their emotions? We all have them: disappointment, frustration, concern, insecurity, or letdown. We can share those with our team and offer them the opportunity to share, too. The power in naming emotions is that by naming them, we allow them to move. We don't get stuck in emotions; we get stuck when we try to deny them or keep them hidden.

Those conversations shift culture. And that's what we really need. The current paradigm in our collective culture around grief isn't serving anyone. The griever feels isolated, confused, and despondent. The supporter feels isolated, scared, and unsure. We can shift that with knowledge and new skills we practice in safe spaces.

Women in leadership positions have an essential role to play. We can start the conversations. We can support people to be more honest. We can step into our powerful ability to hold space without judgment or fixing. Grievers need us. They are suffering. We can make a difference and change that through education and skill development.

Consider this your starting point. You now have some information and understanding you likely didn't have before. Suggestions for where to start. And an invitation to join me on this mission. Join me as an individual changemaker or a leader in your organization. Grievers need you. Organizations need you. Society needs you.

Author Bio

Suzanne Jabour

Suzanne is a grieving mom who has found meaning in her loss through providing grief education – sharing how grief really works and how we can support people experiencing it. Her three-pronged approach is designed to change our response to grief so we do no harm and create connection instead of isolation. She works with grievers to chart their own path through Conscious and Curious Grief Coaching.

Suzanne trains Grief Informed Leaders and transforms businesses through her Grief Resilient Workplace programs. She is available as a speaker to share her story and help normalize grief as a healthy response to losses big and small. She has a BA and BEd and decades of experience as a trainer. She is a certified Grief Educator, and a Transformational Coach and Workshop Leader.

- suzannejabour.com/
- linktr.ee/SuzanneJabourGriefEducation

For Mom. Thank you for encouraging me to be an audacious leader from a very young age.

Mastering the Art of Getting Out of Your Own Way

Lynell Green

"My mission in life is not merely to survive, but to thrive; and to do so with some passion, some compassion, some humor, and some style."
- Maya Angelou

We all have blind spots. There are often things we simply don't see. And it's not like we ignore them; we just don't have the right tools to identify what they are or even where to look. The hard part about that is it's up to you to make those discoveries for yourself.

You have a vision for what your future looks like. Sure some see their futures clearer than others, but we're all on a journey to navigate through our aspirations and realign our lives to have more purpose and clarity. So be honest for a minute. Are you making real progress? We all have that moment of realizing we're not where we anticipated to be, or could have been.

So what's the cause of the setbacks? Well, it's ourselves. You have self-imposed barriers meaning you are most likely the only real obstacle standing in the way of your greatest vision manifesting; and getting out of your own way is an art which requires a specific toolkit.

It's a battle against yourself—one of the toughest opponents you'll ever face. Now I'm a competitive shooter and knife thrower so I know the importance of having an arsenal at your disposal. The right weapon for the job makes all the difference. It dictates how hard the fight will be and whether or not you come out on top. In any battle you actually want to win you have to know your opponent inside and out. Here that means being honest with yourself about who and what you are. Identify where you are today, be clear about the future you're headed toward, and open up to the idea of transforming yourself.

Transformation is a process. When diving into the concept of transformative leadership there is a profound significance on the focus of change. It's not easy and it's not for the faint of heart. When we talk about transformation we're not just talking about improvement or keeping up with trends and patterns. This is a fundamental shift from one state of being to another. On the other side of this shift, who we are—both for ourselves and for others—will change.

Honesty with Our Compass

Your transformation starts with being honest with yourself. Understand the state of your life today and take responsibility for all the choices you made getting here. Don't even dare falling into playing the victim. It'll only make things harder for you, trust me. The following exercises throughout the chapter are to help guide you towards the discovers you need to make:

Self-Reflection Exercise 1

1. Write down all your accomplishments and achievements to date. Next to each one write the lessons and experiences you gained.
2. Write down a list of your skills and competencies. Next to each one write how you learned or honed it.
3. Write down what you wanted to be when you were growing up and what natural talents and gifts fed that idea.
4. As you look at your life today, what is there to celebrate and be grateful for? Write all of those things down.

Think about what you wrote and connect with the idea that you are amazing! It's important to
own our greatness even while on a journey of self-development. Do not see the process as you fixing yourself. You're great in many ways, so all you're doing is adding more to that list. See it as nothing more than expanding your mindset and capacities as a leader.

Self-Reflection Exercise 2

1. Write down instances in both your professional and your personal lives where things didn't go as planned? What did you learn?

2. Do you have any unfinished business from any areas in your past? Any relationships that need attention?
3. Look at a snapshot of your life today and identify any area that isn't working the way you'd like it to? Why do you think it isn't working?

As you're working through these exercises the hope is that you become more aware of actions you need to take. The intention isn't to stir up regrets, resentments, or old frustrations. Look at these things through a new lens, reminding yourself how incredible you are for the things accomplished and listed in exercise one. Also get real with the fact that you can accomplish anything you set your mind to.

Take a minute and list anything you are present to right now as a call to action. You need to face reality, especially as a leader. A compass only tells you where you need to go if the starting point is accurate.

Authenticity is crucial. You're not trying to impress anyone here. This is only between us and we're embarking on this journey together, for you. When we answer questions like the ones above based on what we wish was true rather than what is true it hinders actual progress. Being inauthentic creates what is called cognitive dissonance, inviting it to stay and control our lives. It impacts our ability to execute and take action. We can't move towards our visions if we're confused and refuse to tell ourselves the truth.

Cognitive dissonance is a psychological phenomenon that occurs when we hold conflicting beliefs, attitudes, or values and experience a state of tension between our thoughts and actions. The best remedy to cure this: self-awareness and honesty. And a lot of times that just means a brutal, but necessary, reality-check.

In professional self-development this usually appears as complete confusion. You have no idea why things aren't working or nothing is getting the needle to move. Those blindspots mentioned at the beginning? This is where they are. Clarity prevents confusion... *and getting rid of confusion brings all the issues out of hiding.*

Clarity about the Future

What do you really want? Be straightforward. There are times we aren't making progress or feel stuck because we don't know what we want. We're not clear. You wouldn't go to a restaurant hungry and just stare at the menu then blame the waiter for not bringing out your food. You never told them what you want! So why live life like that? If you never choose then you can't blame anything else. Mastering the art of getting out of your own way requires you make a choice and be clear about what you want right now and for the future. And you can't change your mind constantly, even though many of us do. Again, imagine calling that waiter in the restaurant back every few minutes to tell them you changed your mind and want to order something else. So it should be a no-brainer why your food hasn't come.

When we experience cognitive dissonance, we struggle to make decisions and take action because we're torn between opposing realities. To us, it's easier to do nothing than to make a choice and be wrong. The indecisiveness and reluctance comes from fear. You shouldn't live life confused and afraid anymore.

A lot of us have used public transportation at some point. You need to know where we're going, what bus to get on, and when to get off. Have you ever just sat at a bus stop, never getting on a bus when it stops and just watching them leave until the sun goes down and you're left alone in the dark? Me neither. That's what missing opportunities looks like. Not getting on a bus.

So let's get clear. This next exercise doesn't require you to know how things are going to happen; just say what you want.

Self-Reflection Exercise 3

1. In bullet points, write down what you want in the next three years.
2. From that list identify the things you want in the next twelve months.
3. Looking at the next twelve months, write down which of them you could accomplish in the next three months.

You might be thinking, I've done this before and I still get stumped and never cross the finish line.

As stated earlier, knowing your enemy is only half the battle. You need to be armed with the right weapon and know how to use it. There's a gap between what you want for yourself and your actions that are sabotaging your efforts to get there. A clear disconnect. As leaders we know it's our responsibility to meet challenges and better prepare for the future. The differences between the behaviors and habits needed to do so and our actual behavior is the gap. It's the true target.

Taking on the Gap

So how do you hit your mark on the target? Precision and accuracy. What's intriguing about areas where we need to grow and develop is they often lie outside of our comfort zones. Domains where we're not already excelling or invested hours honing our skills. To achieve genuine transformation you must confront the discomfort in life and leadership. It takes courage to acknowledge our fears of mistakes or wrong choices, and it takes even more to address the gaps in our leadership and take them head-on. This is how we get more precise and accurate.

I invite you to assess your leadership and pinpoint where your gaps are—scrutinize your current methods of doing things and look ahead three to five years. Visualize how you wish to lead. Picture the evolved version of yourself. There should be a clear disparity between your present modus operandi and your future leadership style. You should be able to see which kind of skills are needed to make your dreams a reality. Often when trying to bridge the gap, we find ourselves gravitating towards familiar territories.

For a leader in a business setting a common approach to expansion is all about boosting productivity and efficiency. We explore methods to maximize team output, remain updated on leadership trends, gain deeper industry insights, and establish ourselves as thought leaders. As our responsibilities increase, we delve into areas such as sales, ROI, KPIs, OKRs, diverse business strategies, competitive analysis, and innovative methods to expand market presence. These are valid avenues for growth and development, yet do any of these genuinely catalyze transformation? Do they inspire us to shed the obsolete aspects of ourselves we no longer require because they hold us back? You tell me.

Butterflies are commonly used to illustrate metamorphosis or transformation. The caterpillar going into a cocoon and emerging as a beautiful, new form. But let's dive into the nuances of the journey inside your cocoon. Explore this as our aim is to transform leadership at its core. The goal isn't just to put a cover over something or put on a new exterior. This is transmutation. Complete change into something different and overcoming our self-imposed barriers in the process.

A butterfly begins as a caterpillar. During its caterpillar phase it must shed its skin five times on its path from birth to the chrysalis state. To reach the chrysalis, where transformation transpires, we too must be prepared to shed the dead skin—which could be your income generation methods, lifestyle, work environment, current leadership approach, or community involvement. The manifestations can differ but what matters is our willingness to cast off this figurative dead skin. Remember that maintaining honesty with ourselves is crucial to avoid falling to the cognitive dissonance trap. The trap that gets us stuck in decision-making paralysis and lets fear control our judgment. COgnitive dissonance can also cause emotional discomfort and stress, as we may feel uneasy or guilty about our conflicting thoughts or actions. This emotional distress can lead to avoidance of situations that trigger the dissonance, which in turn impedes personal growth or progress.

Now you're probably asking, why embark on such a journey, is it worth it?

Believe me, I understand. These challenges are formidable for anyone. However, I know the path between where we stand today and our dreams coming true requires surmounting obstacles, winning battles, and moving mountains. Transformation demands discipline and determination. While we may have gotten this far with our current habits and behaviors, we limit ourselves due to what remains neglected. You have to address these areas, reshaping not just our outward presentation but also our perception. Especially our self-perception.

We all know the definition of insanity: doing the same thing and expecting different results. If you want something different for yourself, then you have to do something different. That is why there's so much reflection on our current behavior. The answers and solutions all lie within ironically enough. Shift who you are, clear your vision, and take actions consistent with your future.

Self-Reflection

As I think about the impact cognitive dissonance had on my life and how I allowed it to steer the wheel many times, I realize how devastating it truly is. I notice how it hindered me from moving forward, finding myself stuck in that paralysis trap. I was controlled by fear of making the wrong decision, and that fear quickly overwhelms and takes over.

Self-justification and rationalization reduced the discomfort being in those situations. I'd downplay the importance of my circumstances or even ignore evidence that showed how mistaken my beliefs were. The worst of it all was the excuses. Excuse after excuse for why things weren't as they should've been and placing blame on everything else but myself. That's the mentality you adopt. You become a victim, someone without control over the outcome. The polar opposite of what a leader is. That was the barrier to my personal growth and prevented me from new experiences to learn from.

I avoided feedback that contradicted my beliefs or actions and when confronted with such, I'd completely dismiss it in order to protect myself. There was no courage, just cowardly acts. These defensive responses limited my ability to grow and improve, I wasn't able to become a better person. I had blindspots that aided in creating even more blindspots. That's the opposite direction with self-awareness, and I missed valuable opportunities.

This shaped my limited perspective on the world. I only sought out information that confirmed my existing beliefs. Exposure was avoided subconsciously at that point. No diversity in viewpoints, no nuance, no new information that could challenge or enrich my understanding of things. I was stuck. All development was basically frozen.

This is why I'm making these efforts with you. To help you advance and overcome cognitive dissonance. We're arming you with the tools to stay out of traps and work towards your dreams and aspirations, confidently. Engage in introspection, seek feedback from others, embrace change and have the courage to confront conflict. Break free from cognitive dissonance's grip and realize the importance of self-awareness. Enjoy the process and embark on the journey to transform into your greatest potential.

Author Bio

Lynell Green

Lynell Green is a highly accomplished strategic management consultant and executive coach, renowned for her expertise in unleashing leadership potential and fostering strategic growth. With over 40 years of experience, Lynell has successfully worked with an impressive roster of clients, including industry leaders at Meta, Netflix, X, Microsoft, and Hilton. Her unique combination of skills, including accounting, corporate management, and teaching leadership programs, allows her to provide invaluable insights and guidance to her clients.

Lynell's ability to understand complex business strategies, navigate organizational dynamics, and develop effective leaders has consistently resulted in transformative outcomes for her clients. Through her coaching, Lynell empowers leaders to inspire and unleash the leadership potential around them, creating a ripple effect of growth and success throughout their organizations.

• lynellsplace.com/

To my dad

Raising Awareness:

The Imperative for Health Equity

Debra Duran

I became a nurse in 1988. I was a young mother at the time and very naïve regarding anything outside of my immediate circle. Growing up in a poor suburb of Los Angeles, everyone I knew looked like me, and spoke like me. Most of us were sons or daughters of immigrants from Mexico. It was comfortable.

Despite growing up in what was considered a gang-infested neighborhood, I recall walking alone to and from school and not feeling afraid of being shot, stabbed, or killed. The biggest threat at that time was kidnapping, and I at least knew better than to get into a car with anybody I didn't know.

At sixteen, I found myself pregnant. Again, being naïve, I thought the best thing would be for me to marry my then-boyfriend. Since I always excelled in school, the fact that I had a baby did not deter me from wanting to go to college. In fact, it made me want that more. Now, I knew I had to do whatever possible to be a good provider for my family.

Going to the University of Southern California opened my eyes to many new experiences. For example, in classrooms, I was introduced to people from non-Mexican communities, but that exposure was minimal since I rarely interacted with anyone from school outside of the classroom. Because I was a mom and not the typical carefree single person, my focus was to finish school, get my degree, pass my state exam, find full-time employment, and support my family. It was a very narrow focus.

At that time, I hadn't traveled outside my immediate neighborhood except to visit family in Mexico. I had no clue how people lived in surrounding cities and states of the U.S., and I'm ashamed to acknowledge that I had little interest in exploring anything outside of my comfort zone, my community.

Even after working as a Registered Nurse, I elected to work in my same community, serving people who looked and sounded just like me. Fortunately, working for the local government gave me the opportunity to be promoted to positions that required me to serve all underserved populations in Los Angeles (not just my own immediate community). I began to witness the effects of poverty and how disenfranchised communities were experiencing illness. I began to learn and understand how certain people of color experience higher rates of morbidity and mortality compared to their white counterparts. And still, I was naïve.

It wasn't until well into my forties that I began to open my eyes and my mind. My growing children were pivotal to this expansion of vision that I experienced. My children spoke to me about climate change, Bernie Sanders, student loan debt, unaffordable housing, and, yes, racial disparities. As I listened to their fresh perspectives, I began to see that I had been so focused on my immediate circle that I failed to recognize they were living in a world different from mine.

I didn't have any student debt, for example. My undergraduate degree was completely paid for by grants and scholarships. I hadn't worried about global warming in my youth. I was able to purchase a home for a reasonable amount of money compared to my income—something that many can no longer do today, especially in California. And while I always knew poor people, and specifically people of color, fared poorly in health, I didn't pay attention to the "why."

In nursing school, we were taught that patients were what was called "non-compliant" or a "poor historian." Always with an undertone of judgment, we blamed them for their poor outcomes. And while I am a proponent of holding people accountable for their actions, I certainly know now—what most of us know now—is that when the cards are stacked against you, your experience in life is focused on survival. When having to meet the most basic needs of food and shelter is a struggle, how can one be "compliant" with taking medicines that one can't afford and exercising in a neighborhood that isn't safe? People's experiences vastly differ based on socioeconomic status, ZIP code, childhood trauma, post-traumatic stress, etc.

Health Equity

From the lens of a nurse, I know that Black mothers suffer higher mortality rates than non-Black mothers. I know that Hispanics had the highest rates of COVID deaths compared to others. I know that people in the LGBTQ community report avoiding medical appointments because they feel unwelcome. I know that people who need a healthcare language interpreter are often faced with delays and, therefore, volunteer a family member as an interpreter—even though that very fact can bias the information that the patient is willing to share due to privacy concerns.

Consider how access to health care is affected by not having a car to get around in. Consider what your experience would be like if you had to take three buses to get to one medical appointment. If the bus is running late, you will miss the appointment you waited weeks or months to schedule. All of these are factors related to health equity. Things that many of us take for granted, such as a roof over our heads, adequate food on the table, a car (or maybe two), paid leave to use for medical appointments, etc. People of color and living in dense, poor populations do not have the same access to health care that most of us do. They rely on public services that are often overburdened with demand exceeding supply.

My healthcare experience may sometimes be difficult to navigate, and yet I know what to do to advocate for myself and my family. When you don't speak the language, don't get paid to attend a medical appointment, take several buses to get to one appointment only to not understand what the doctor is telling you, and can't afford to pay for the medicines they prescribed, what are the chances that you will achieve wellness? How privileged I am compared to them. How is that equitable healthcare? The truth is, that it isn't. How can we, as a society, make it so that we can even the playing field? Break down barriers that contribute to people being more likely to suffer disease and disability. Not all things are created equitably .

Biases

We all have biases. Whether we acknowledge that we do or not, we all have them. Some are implicit. Some are explicit. They are so ingrained that often we are completely unaware of them unless we are paying close attention or someone calls us out. We may not realize that a response was based on bias.

For example, I was at an airport this week. There was a Black woman in line ahead of me and a Black man behind her. The TSA worker asked the woman if they were together. She replied no and proceeded to ask him why he thought they were together, to which he replied, "I don't know." He likely assumed they were a couple because they were both Black and appeared to be in the same age range. Similarly, several female physician colleagues shared that when they walked the hallways of a hospital or entered a patient's room, they were often mistaken for a nurse by the patient or the patient's family.

So, how do these seemingly innocuous biases affect how we provide health care? Maybe because we make assumptions about a patient's intelligence based on their mastery of the English language. Perhaps we judge a patient with diabetes as being non-compliant with their prescribed diet, exercise, and medication treatment plan without knowing that they are likely going to lose their housing and don't have enough money to buy food for the week before their next paycheck. How can they focus on adhering to their doctor's plan if their basic needs for food and shelter are not met? Is it okay as a society to turn a blind eye to folks who are suffering when we live in one of the wealthiest countries? Is it not in everyone's best interest to help each other for the greater good?

Disparities

I witness disparities in treatment all the time. Likely, you do, too. Does an adult White male who comes from generational wealth, has a few college degrees, and works in finance have the same access to healthcare and the same opportunity to achieve optimum health outcomes compared to a Black male working a job that does not pay for personal time off, living in a densely populated part of the city? Their access to healthcare and their interactions with doctors and nurses will be different, and whether we want to admit it or not, the White male will come up faring much better. The healthcare professionals will more quickly respond to health concerns voiced by the White male. People from the Black community often report that their concerns are not taken seriously by doctors. This can lead to delays in diagnosis and poorer outcomes.

I understand that my saying this may incite a reaction in some readers, and they may view this as a political statement. I assure you this is not coming from a place of politics. It is the cruel reality of the world. And this is everyone's problem. Because one way or another, as a society, we will pay a price for not addressing disparities and inequities. As taxpayers, citizens, and humans, there is a cost to not addressing these matters. Disparities in treatment mean that some people get better treatment than others. Couldn't we make it so that everyone has access to basic human needs and is equally taken seriously?

Even people who come from wealth, are highly educated, and serve our country, etc., can be one medical emergency away from bankruptcy and homelessness. So, are we okay with looking the other way until or unless it happens to us? I'm not saying I have the answers to these difficult questions; I'm just trying to raise awareness, provoke thought, shed some light, and see if, as a nation, we can come up with solutions we can feel good about.

Open Minds

I realize that some of you reading this may experience what I'm writing with an impassioned response. The topic of health equity and disparities and biases can do that. All I am suggesting is that we keep an open mind and study the research. Real research. Academic studies that are peer-reviewed, as opposed to what we hear and see on the news or in social media or what someone tells us. I encourage fact-finding and studying statistics. Let that be what informs you.

Political vs. Basic Human Rights

Some may say that health equity is a political issue. Is it? Isn't access to healthcare a basic right? Shouldn't all our children, aunts, uncles, and parents have access to health care? Shouldn't we all be concerned about the fact that when people suffer, we all end up suffering the consequences of that? So, if we care about humankind, is that a political matter? What I would offer is that we all keep an open mind, see the suffering of others, and care enough to take steps to address it.

I hope you, the reader, will have your interest piqued about health equity. You may ask, what can we do to address health equity? What will it take to help others? There is no simple solution. First, we have to accept and acknowledge that this is our reality. Addressing systemic barriers and biases will take years to change. What I would offer is that we stay curious.

Take small actions that come from a place of curiosity instead of coming from a place of judgment toward those who are disenfranchised. Ask open-ended questions that lead to transformation. For example, "How might we improve ....?" Pay attention to interactions you witness and your own behavior to see if you spot any unaddressed biases. Then, address them through nonjudgmental conversations with others or yourself.

Attend local council meetings. Educate yourself on these matters and then share that knowledge with others who are in a position to make change. Hospital boards, school boards, and almost any setting where people have the power to break down barriers.

For example, if transportation is a barrier to getting to medical appointments for some, can we lobby for non-emergency medical transportation in that community that is low- or no-cost? Eventually, perhaps we will pass laws and fund unique programs to help those in need. I hope you can do the research and learn more about what the evidence teaches us. In doing so, at a minimum, we will have a heightened awareness of the situation at hand and hopefully begin to work toward solutions.

As for me, I'm speaking about the challenges of health equity wherever I go. Spreading knowledge and also respecting when I have an audience that is not open to the conversation. I focus on those who are willing to keep an open mind. In the future, I intend to launch a podcast where people can have a safe place to discuss these matters, focus on how to spread knowledge and search for scalable ways to spread change. So, stay tuned for that!

In gratitude,

Debra Duran

Author Bio

Debra Duran

Debra is a retired Chief Nursing Officer with over thirty years working as a nurse in underserved communities in Los Angeles County. Ms. Duran witnessed first-hand the effects of health disparities in the communities she served. She is passionate about patient advocacy and spreading awareness around health equity. She is a leader that galvanizes teams to work toward a common goal that is mission driven.

Ms. Duran successfully led programs that improved outcomes for high-risk patient populations. Now, in retirement she is pursuing work in logistics and still remains committed to raising awareness around health equity. She plans to pursue hosting a podcast on the subject matter to have open dialogue related to health equity with leaders working to make changes that support the health of all people.

- linkedin.com/in/debra-duran-b9134717b/

My chapter is dedicated to all of the women around the world who are embracing the courage and tenacity needed to develop self-leadership and step up into leadership roles in their family, community, and workplace. Let's create positive change together.

The Evolution of Leadership:

Women Catalyzing Change

Cathy Derksen

"Daring leadership is ultimately about serving others, not ourselves. Daring leaders must care for and be connected to the people they lead. Daring leaders work to make sure people can be themselves and feel a sense of belonging."

- Brené Brown from Dare to Lead

My vision and definition of leadership have been expanded and deepened by the amazing women I've met in the past few years. Immersing myself in several women-run organizations has opened my eyes to the changes women are creating in leadership. I've met so many women who are frustrated and disillusioned by the archaic models of leadership traditionally seen in so many organizations.

Women are transforming leadership at every level in business and community. Over time, we have been replacing the good ol' boys' club with a fresh new look and feel. Women are taking on leadership from new perspectives with new strategies and styles.

Collaboration and mentorship have replaced traditional competition and the 'survival of the fittest' mentality. As diversity, equity, and inclusion have become mainstream conversations, we have embraced a wide range of approaches to leadership.

As I look back over my decades in the workforce, there are many examples of good leaders as well as ones who had a very destructive impact on their staff and clients. My original career was in healthcare. I specialized in clinical genetics and spent 25 years working in hospital labs and public education.

My second career was in financial planning, working in large banks and investment companies. When I chose to leave these employers, in both cases, my decision was greatly influenced by the negative impact of working under destructive leadership. I was dealing with physical and mental health issues associated with toxic work environments.

During those two chapters of my career, I didn't see an option for bringing change to those workplaces, and I didn't feel I had any power or voice to impact the leadership model I worked under. The only option I could see for saving myself from the chronic health issues brought on due to the stress of working in these situations was to remove myself from the environment.

My career in healthcare and my career in finance were both cut short as a direct result of leadership models that treated employees as little more than a cog in the wheel of a large organization.

In 2020, I made the massive decision to leave behind the life of being employed by these large companies. I chose to set out on my own to create a career that met my needs and brought joy to my life. My journey as an entrepreneur has had its share of ups and downs, but the lessons I've learned along the way have been life changing.

I've witnessed many women who have chosen to either step up into a role that allows them to make changes in their current workplace or have walked away from these organizations to create a new business that exemplifies the values and behaviors they choose to live by. They are not just taking a seat at the leadership table to create change, they are starting a whole new table that allows them to set the ground rules.

In these new leadership models, the focus is on tapping into the strengths of each member of the organization and replacing competition with collaboration. These changes allow each member to feel valued and respected. These leadership styles encourage team members to feel connected and supported, consequentially leading to more productivity and less staff turnover.

Honoring diversity in the workplace has also become a critical factor in creating more success on many levels. A wide variety of perspectives, attitudes, and lived experiences allows a team to be more creative and incorporate new ideas into their decision-making process.

Another significant trend in leadership styles that has been part of this evolution is the shift from looking at leadership as a top-down hierarchy. The old model, having one person at the top with all of the control, has shifted to a model that sees many team members having various levels of leadership opportunities in their jobs.

In bringing together the team of authors in this book, my goal is to spotlight and highlight a small group of women who are transforming leadership in business and community. Their stories demonstrate their journey and how they became inspired to take on leadership roles in their life at work and at home. My vision for this book is to inform and inspire women around the world to take on their own journey as leaders in every aspect of their lives.

As I've taken my own path as a leader, I have developed many new skills and learned lessons that will impact the rest of my life. I have left behind the work environments that had me feeling disrespected and taken advantage of, and I've developed my own business that allows me to create the community and atmosphere that supports me and my team to excel in our passions.

I'd love to share a few of the lessons I learned along the way with the hope they will help you, the reader, have an easier road to creating your own success in life.

Lead with your own unique style. Of course, we all have skills to develop as we become leaders, but the lessons we learn should be focused on developing and enhancing our own style. When I first stepped into leadership roles, I was told I needed to be big and flashy. Whenever I attempted to develop that style, it felt unauthentic and uncomfortable. I learned that being myself and sharing my passion as authentically as possible is key.

Step out of the box and do things your way. Most of my life, I believed my career path needed to be made up of preexisting job descriptions. Now, I know that being creative in bringing your vision to life is so much more fun. The work I'm doing now, creating these multi-author book projects, was birthed from my passion for supporting women in sharing their stories and stepping into new possibilities in life. There were no guidelines to follow or job descriptions to stick with. My vision became my reality. Now, the work I'm doing impacts women around the world and shares voices that haven't been heard.

Build a community of support and encouragement. As you step into new areas of leadership, you will go through many challenges, and you'll need to navigate many obstacles along the way. It is critical to have a community around you that will provide a safe space to share your challenges, vent your frustrations, and remind you that you're not alone. Together, we can lift each other.

Be open to collaboration and mentorship. Find ways that you and your community can work together and provide complimentary services. You can achieve a new level of success by bringing together each person's expertise.

Be courageous and bold. Creating change in the world always comes with making major decisions and taking action in ways that aren't familiar or comfortable. Step into these challenges with confidence. Feel the fear and do it anyway.

Dream big. Allow yourself to create a big vision of the future you aim to create without the limiting beliefs that have kept you playing small.

Be a role model for others. As you step up into various levels of leadership in your life other people will take notice. By stepping into a new version of yourself, you are giving other women the motivation and example to follow in your footsteps. Sharing your story and being open to supporting others creates a ripple effect of positive impacts on the world.

Self-leadership needs to be the foundation of all leadership possibilities. Learning how to manage yourself, your mindset, your emotional intelligence, and your social responses, will establish your strength as a leader of.

I love this quote by Buckminster Fuller:

"You never change things by fighting the existing reality. To change something, build a new model that makes the existing model obsolete."

Let's work together to create a model of leadership that brings positive change to the world. You can create this change at every level of your life, whether at work, at home, in your community, or within your own personal journey.

Author Bio

Cathy Derksen

Cathy Derksen is the founder of her company, Inspired Tenacity Global Solutions Inc.. She is a Disruptor and Catalyst dedicated to improving the lives of the women in her community and around the world. Cathy helps women rediscover their brilliance, find their voice and create a life they love.

A decade ago, Cathy transformed her career from working in Medical Genetics for 25 years to financial planning so that she could focus on helping women create personal success. Over the years, Cathy has followed her passion for learning and has become certified in counselling, leadership, success principles, and strategies for overcoming limiting beliefs and mindset. Her programs at Inspired Tenacity allow her to blend all of her skills to amplify the impact of her work.

Cathy is now an international speaker and 15x #1 bestselling author. She has created a platform for women to share their wisdom and inspiring stories in collaborative books like this one. She takes them from chapter concept to bestselling author in a simple, exciting process.

Cathy has two children (31 and 30 yrs) and 2 fur-babies. She lives near Vancouver, Canada

She enjoys spending time in nature, travelling, meeting new people, and connecting with her global community.

- inspiredtenacity.com
- linkedin.com/in/cathyderkseninspiredtenacity

To Suzanne, my coach and guide: Thank you for helping me create a path forward and for always believing in my potential. I'm grateful I didn't have to walk this journey alone!

From Mountains to Milestones: Navigating Leadership in Uncharted Territory

Kolleen Chesley

It was April 2021, and I was on a trail in Red Rock Canyon, just minutes from Las Vegas. During that time, I spent weekends on adventures and discovering my love for hiking. The trails and mountains became my happy place, where I processed and learned valuable lessons—including a major breakthrough that changed my trajectory and that of the nonprofit I founded.

Hiking provided time to think. Our excursions lasted for hours, sometimes with climbs over 500 feet. I hiked with my husband and dog, who both raced up the trail. I followed behind, easily distracted and appreciating nature. I'd pause to admire the views, snap photos, and become immersed in the scenery.

With most of my adult life spent in Florida, I hadn't explored mountains until now. I was fascinated by the ever-changing landscape—each step and gained elevation revealed a new view. Being captivated by the change of perspective, I wanted to capture every moment. Admittedly, the frequent photo breaks also helped me catch my breath, as I was a bit out of shape. My husband and I would only talk at the summit, with my journey mainly spent in solitude, winding through switchbacks and taking in the breathtaking vistas. Deep thinking also occupied me during the hikes.

We had been in Nevada for four months and had settled in well. Most of the city had reopened after the pandemic, but it was far from "normal." Many places had mask requirements, limited hours, and reduced staffing. The limited hustle and bustle made it easier for me to learn the city. Before long, I was comfortable navigating around.

Before setting up our second home in Vegas, I hadn't lived in a new city in over 35 years. Growing up, having an Air Force dad meant frequent moves every four years. In adulthood, I had settled into one familiar city, Pensacola, Florida. The addition of Vegas was refreshing, allowing me to explore new surroundings and have fresh adventures.

The move was also a bit of a test for us, as I allowed my husband the opportunity to pursue a larger sales territory while we maintained our Florida home, too. I flew back and forth every other month—spending part-time in Pensacola for in-person activities and working remotely the rest of the time. While in Vegas, I continued my work with Powerful Women of the Gulf Coast (PWGC), the nonprofit I founded in 2004.

The mission of PWGC is to promote and advance women in business. Prior to the pandemic, we were on a growth trajectory with membership and fundraising. We had long dreamed of expanding beyond Florida, and this was an opportunity to explore that. The pandemic had certainly impacted the organization, as it had everyone. However, we remained optimistic about the future.

Vegas is a large city with over two million residents, and I was thrilled to find over fifteen active Chambers of Commerce, including two focused on women. There were numerous other organizations for women in business, including large conferences and expos that would restart soon.

In contrast, Pensacola's population of 300,000 offered fewer dedicated programs and opportunities for women in business. I was elated to learn from Vegas' wealth of experience and expertise, with the opportunity to bring best practices back to support the women in the Florida Gulf Coast area.

Despite my eagerness, the pandemic limited my exploration to virtual meetings and events, as in-person networking remained paused for the entire nine months we were there.

Instead, I researched and connected virtually from Vegas, expanding my Florida contact base. I signed up for virtual conferences, webinars, and summits focusing on deep analysis for women in business. I attended webinars on the pandemic's economic impact from the UN, McKinsey, and PBS. I read analyses from the US Chamber, *Forbes*, and the Census Bureau. I started to see the larger picture of the pandemic's devastating effects on women in business. And I realized this was a pattern my gender had likely seen before.

A commonly reported statistic is that one in four women reconsidered their corporate positions during the pandemic.[1] Through

---

1   https://www.uschamber.com/workforce/data-deep-dive-a-decline-of-women-in-the-workforce

compiling articles and references, a larger picture emerged—the pandemic affected women-owned businesses disproportionately,[2] with higher closure rates[3] and slower reopenings[4] compared to male-owned businesses. Article after article clearly documented the national and global impacts.

As I researched, I wondered how these statistics applied to the women I served and recalled conversations I had with our members. Throughout the pandemic, I reached out multiple times to check in and provide support for them. These conversations often went beyond surface-level discussions, and I wanted to truly understand how each member was faring and how their businesses were impacted.

The conversations were positive, with members praising PWGC's support and appreciative of being contacted. We were known as a strong networking organization, and members spoke of the confidence, friendships, and business partnerships forged through our events. They discussed leaning on and supporting each other in ways far beyond our events and gatherings. Our efforts had clearly created meaningful impacts.

However, though we provided valuable networking opportunities, most members' businesses still suffered. As business struggles were common during the pandemic, I began to see direct parallels between our members' stories and the disproportionate impacts on women-owned versus male-owned businesses.

I remember a conversation with a salon business owner who really struggled during the shutdown. She had exhausted her resources, trying to pivot without success. Confused by the changing Payment Protection Program (PPP) loan rules, she lacked a knowledgeable advocate to guide her and didn't apply for either round of grant money despite having definite business losses.

She was proactive and watched webinars and news releases to try and understand the process. After meeting with one professional who said she didn't qualify, she stopped, thinking that person was thoroughly informed. Unfortunately, her business has since shut down.

---

2   https://www.uschamber.com/workforce/special-report-women-owned-small-businesses-during-covid-19
3   https://www.sbc.senate.gov/public/_cache/files/b/9/b99ffab8-b62a-48e1-95ba-b14c5451880b/D779F6653743546214AD6E09EAED29F7.women-entrepreneurship-report.pdf
4   https://www.theatlantic.com/international/archive/2020/03/feminism-womens-rights-coronavirus-covid19/608302/

I remember thinking back and seeing this directly aligning with the research I found that talked about women being great relationship builders but noticeably reluctant to actually leverage those relationships in times of need. Could we have helped her had she spoken up?

I spoke with a retail boutique owner who experienced major business losses, and her employees were affected. Though connected enough to navigate PPP, her business didn't qualify. It turns out she had been paying her staff and sinking all her profits back into the company, not paying herself or paying herself very little. So, when she had to prove her own loss of income to qualify for PPP, she couldn't. Why do we women still not pay ourselves what we're worth? This hit me hard, as her story wasn't the only member who shared a similar struggle.

Many of our women-owned business members suffered, and their stories echoed national research. Some lacked the knowledge to pivot online when the pandemic hit. Others struggled to navigate the complex PPP process or balance running a business from their kitchen while homeschooling their children. Companies in Florida faced pressure to stay open, regardless of comfort levels. I wondered how many Florida Gulf Coast women business leaders suffered in silence, their stories of struggle, lack of knowledge, and overwhelming pressures reflecting broader national trends.

All of this weighed heavy when I set out to hike that warm, sunny Saturday in April 2021. We set out on a familiar trail in Red Rock Canyon, just minutes from our apartment. Unlike the winding mountain trails, where the scenery constantly shifts as you gain elevation, this ridgeline hike allowed us to see the path ahead. I loved the expansive views—you could clearly see where you were going, rather than the surprises around each bend on our usual mountain treks.

Studying the trail map, I saw this hike as an opportunity for clarity. I love setting mental intentions and then seeing what thoughts come forward. As I walked, lost in thought, I replayed conversations with members and reflected on research about the pandemic's impact on women in business. While I often used these hikes to ponder life in general, this time, the clarity of the path ahead mirrored the insights emerging—*women in business needed more support.*

By Monday morning, something had shifted. I woke at my usual 5:00 a.m. to be ready for the East Coast workday, a routine I hadn't struggled with—until this Monday. Mentally exhausted, I dreaded the early start, a stark contrast to my previous mornings.

As with any bad morning, I pressed on; however, I still struggled for the rest of the day. By day's end, I hoped it was just an off day—perhaps I needed more rest.

The next day wasn't any better. I gave myself a break, canceling non-essential meetings and appointments. In the past, reducing my workload had provided reprieve and energy. But after a week, the exhaustion persisted, with no surge of renewed energy.

In the following weeks, I eliminated any non-essential work. As an organization, we reduced activities and events, allowing me to step back. I thought further reducing my workload would reignite my spark, but it didn't.

I loved my work with PWGC, but the organization I had founded and been running since 2004 was suddenly... a chore. For the first time, I felt no drive to help others—I was in total burnout. I later learned I had likely unknowingly been driving myself to this condition for years.

What I learned about burnout is that it's not simple. I was familiar with the topic, as our PWGC events featured speakers covering burnout, which can be common for high-achieving women.

What I thought was burnout turned out to be just one type of burnout. I knew about exhaustion burnout caused by overwhelming workloads, but that wasn't me. Despite the pandemic pivot, my workload had actually decreased since 2021.

I also knew about depletion burnout caused by a lack of self-care. But that wasn't me either—I was ascending mountains, eating healthier, and enjoying daily swims in our apartment pool, a luxury I didn't have in Florida. I worked limited hours and refreshed my energy daily with new adventures and fun.

My burnout stemmed from a misalignment between my beliefs about our nonprofit's impact on women-owned businesses and the reality I uncovered. For years, our organization grew, with high membership and event attendance—it looked like we were making a difference. But, the research and member stories revealed that this wasn't enough when the crisis hit.

We had become experts at networking, but women in business needed far more support. This cognitive dissonance, this disconnect between my activity and the actual impact, weighed heavily. The realization hit me hard, like a brick to the face. My version of burnout arose from this misalignment, not from overwhelming workloads or lack of self-care. This was a different type of burnout, rooted in the gap between my beliefs and the harsh realities women entrepreneurs faced.

After months of trying to pull myself out of burnout, I reached out for help—hiring a coach has been invaluable. I also consulted medical professionals, a therapist, and a health coach, exploring modalities like EMDR, homeopathy, and self-hypnosis. I learned about perimenopause (yes, I'm there too), biorhythms, astrology, and leaned into self-assessments. This mental work slowly began to pay off as I regained energy for my role. If my story resonates with you, I highly encourage seeking a coach to support you through burnout.

My burnout and the awareness it brought led to significant changes. Our members' stories and my own experience shifted my perspective—instead of more networking, we needed to address the deeper, hidden issues that hold back women in business. This realization sparked a fundamental shift in our nonprofit's focus.

I took each member's story, extracted core issues, and compared patterns. Many similarities emerged—women across various industries told similar stories and suffered in the same ways. I was astounded by these repetitions.

Analyzing the stories, I identified four key issue categories. Aligning this with my research on the pandemic's impact on women-owned businesses, I found direct parallels—the local challenges mirrored the national trends. Though our nonprofit only operated regionally, the women's stories echoed the broader realities revealed in my comprehensive research. From this realization, we created four pillars representing the key challenges women face. We outlined the issues in each pillar, identified the deeper impact, and designed programs to help women overcome these barriers. This insight drove changes to align our events and initiatives with these critical focus areas.

The first pillar, the **Power Pillar**, addresses how women struggle to quantify their worth, leading to confidence issues, imposter syndrome, and mindset challenges—a story echoed by many members. This critical issue became the foundation, guiding our vision as we continued to focus on empowering women to overcome these additional barriers.

The remaining pillars are:

- **Wisdom Pillar:** Women struggle due to unrealistic social media portrayals and expectations around work-life balance, obscuring authentic success stories.
- **Givers Pillar:** Mean girl dynamics, both external and internal, persist as women hold themselves and others back by not embracing authenticity.
- **Community Pillar:** Women leaders often feel isolated, underscoring the invaluable support found in sharing struggles, seeking inspiration, and learning from others.

These four pillars now guide our efforts to address the core challenges women face in business, aligning our efforts with our impact.

As I reflect, it's been nearly three years since that hike in Red Rock Canyon. Personally, we've consolidated back to one Florida household, and my hiking is now limited to flatter landscapes. I still connect with nature, but on a sandy beach, and sometimes still in hiking boots. However, my mental work remains a priority. Though not cured of long-term burnout, I daily endeavor to ensure my actions drive meaningful impact, staying focused on fulfilling work rather than just checking boxes or serving others at my own expense.

PWGC continued its transition as we merged with LeadHERship Global in August 2023. We have since spun off a new 501c3 with the same mission, Powerful Women Collective. This organization continues to be a lighthouse for Gulf Coast businesswomen.

My personal trajectory changed as well, and the merger brought a leadership position for me to be supportive in bigger ways and help women worldwide.

As I continue navigating my journey on mountain trails or sandy beaches and also in women's leadership, I'm reminded of the resilience within us all. Lessons from solitary reflections to eye-opening conversations have lit the path forward. While the road may be challenging, I'm committed to supporting women, dismantling barriers, and fostering a community of support and solidarity.

Together, embracing our grit and tenacity, we have the power to transform businesses, communities, and the world. Whether in hiking boots, heels, or barefoot, I'll face the journey with courage and determination, knowing the summit is within reach, one step at a time.

Author Bio

Kolleen Chesley

Kolleen Chesley is the visionary behind Powerful Women Synergized, a movement committed to closing the economic power gap for women entrepreneurs. Her mission was sparked by the July 2023 "Women's Small Business Ownership and Entrepreneurship Report," which revealed that equal participation by women in entrepreneurship could boost global GDP by $5 to $7 trillion. Despite this potential, systemic and self-imposed barriers continue to limit women's ability to thrive in business.

Recognizing the solvability of this gap, Kolleen launched Powerful Women Synergized to address these inequities head-on. Her consultancy equips women CEOs, founders, and entrepreneurs with the tools they need to succeed—streamlining operations, making data-driven decisions, and uncovering hidden revenue streams. Kolleen is passionate about creating a support system that empowers women to break through obstacles that prevent them from reaching their full potential.

The mission of Powerful Women Synergized isn't just about improving business processes—it's about rewriting the narrative for women in leadership and ensuring their rightful place in the global economy. Kolleen's approach is both strategic and personal, grounded in the belief that every woman-led business can become a powerhouse of innovation, growth, and impact with the right support.

Through her work, Kolleen helps women move beyond the barriers that hold them back, unlocking their potential to make a profound economic impact. Her goal is to see a world where women are key drivers of global economic success. The time to close the gap is now, and Kolleen is dedicated to leading that charge.

• closethepowergap.com

Dedication: To you, the courageous woman ready to step into your expertise, increase your success, and lead with purpose. Your dedication, intelligence, and passion are shaping the future, breaking barriers, and inspiring others to create lasting impact in the world.

Ready to Be an Expert? Increase Your Success and Significance Now!

Kathleen Caldwell

When you become an expert in your career or business, you don't just participate in the market—you shape it, redefine it, and lead it with unparalleled confidence.

You've devoted yourself to your career, showcasing intelligence, talent, and commitment. You've refined your skills and mastered the art of coaching, consulting, or advising. Yet, one crucial step remains to truly excel in your business and career—becoming an expert.

By transforming your leadership approach, you can uncover new opportunities to drive positive change in both business and community. Effective leaders inspire innovation, foster collaboration, and create environments where everyone can thrive. Embracing this transformative journey not only enhances your professional growth but also empowers you to make a lasting impact on the world around you.

Why You Must Become an Expert Now

Becoming an expert means having extensive knowledge and experience in your field and being recognized as a leader and authority in your industry. This distinction sets you apart, giving you credibility, trustworthiness, and influence that can significantly elevate your professional standing. With expertise, you position yourself as a go-to resource, enhancing your reputation and opening up numerous opportunities for career growth and development.

In addition, expertise allows you to command higher rates for your services, attract high-profile clients, and secure prestigious speaking engagements and media appearances. For women who are coaches, consultants, and trusted advisors, embracing and showcasing your expertise is even more imperative. Women often face societal, cultural, and systemic barriers in the workplace and business world, such as gender biases, unequal opportunities, and limited access to certain networks. By becoming an expert, women can overcome these obstacles, break through the glass ceiling, and achieve success on their own terms.

Moreover, the journey to becoming an expert involves continuous learning and growth. This means staying updated with the latest trends, consistently improving your skills, and gaining new qualifications or certifications that enhance your knowledge base. Engaging in professional development activities, attending industry conferences, and networking with peers are also essential steps in solidifying your expert status.

By visibly demonstrating your expertise, you inspire other women to aspire to higher positions and contribute to a culture of excellence and equality. It also fosters a sense of empowerment and confidence, encouraging more women to pursue leadership roles and advocate for themselves and others in their industry. In essence, expertise is not just about personal achievement; it is about paving the way for future generations of women to thrive and excel.

Furthermore, as an expert, you have the platform to influence and drive change within your industry. You can contribute to shaping policies, mentor upcoming professionals, and be a voice in critical discussions. This enhances your own career and has a broader impact on the industry as a whole, promoting innovation and progress. By setting a high standard of excellence, you help create an environment where talent is recognized and valued, irrespective of gender.

Becoming an expert is a powerful tool for career advancement, personal empowerment, and social change. It requires dedication, continuous learning, and a proactive approach to overcoming challenges. For women, in particular, achieving expert status opens doors to new opportunities and paves the way for future generations to follow. Embrace the journey to expertise and make a lasting impact in your field and beyond.

How To Become An Expert

Becoming an expert doesn't happen overnight; it takes time, effort, dedication, and continuous learning. Mastery in any field requires persistent practice, the ability to learn from failures, and a deep commitment to honing your skills. It's a journey filled with challenges and rewards, where every experience contributes to your growth and expertise. To become an expert, you must:

- **Identify Your Niche:** Begin by pinpointing a specific area within your field where you possess extensive knowledge and experience. This could be a particular industry, such as technology or healthcare, or a specific type of client you excel in working with, like corporations, small businesses, or nonprofits. By focusing on a niche, you not only stand out and establish yourself as an expert but also tailor your services to meet that market's unique needs. This specialization helps you attract the right clients, build a strong reputation, and create more targeted, effective marketing strategies. Additionally, it can lead to more significant opportunities for growth and collaboration within your chosen niche.
- **Develop Your Point of View:** Having a unique perspective and point of view is vital in today's competitive landscape. Identify your unique take on industry topics and issues and use it to differentiate yourself from others. Take time to analyze different opinions, gather insights from various sources, and critically assess the information you encounter. Reflect on your experiences, values, and knowledge to shape an informed and original viewpoint. Once you have formed your own perspective, consistently express it through your content and communications, such as blog posts, social media updates, and speaking engagements. This will help to establish yourself as a thought leader in your field and build a loyal audience that values your insights and opinions.
- **Collaborate with Other Experts:** Working with other experts can help you learn more by sharing insights and experiences. This collaboration can also enable you to reach a larger audience through combined networks. By pooling resources and expertise, you can tackle more complex problems and innovate in ways you might not have achieved alone. Ultimately, this approach builds beneficial relationships and fosters a community of shared knowledge and mutual support, allowing for continuous growth and development in your field.
- **Continuously Evaluate and Improve:** Regularly assess your skills and knowledge through self-reflection and performance reviews. Take the time to analyze your strengths

and weaknesses and set specific, measurable goals for improvement. Seek feedback from clients, peers, and mentors to identify areas for growth and development, and use this input to implement meaningful changes in your approach. Additionally, enroll in groups, masterminds, courses, and workshops to stay current with the latest industry trends and advancements. Consistent effort toward self-improvement will not only enhance your professional capabilities but also increase your confidence and effectiveness in your role.

- **Share Your Knowledge:** Write informative and engaging articles or blogs about your expertise, providing detailed explanations, practical tips, and real-world examples that resonate with your audience. Participate in webinars or podcasts to reach a broader audience and share valuable insights, offering your unique perspectives and solutions to common problems. Speak at industry events and conferences to establish yourself as a thought leader, and take advantage of these opportunities to network with like-minded professionals, exchange ideas, and collaborate on innovative projects.

Breaking the Gender Barrier

In many industries, women are increasingly stepping into leadership roles and demonstrating their expertise. This shift is helping to break down historical biases and reshape societal norms and professional structures. Women with equal or superior qualifications and experience are now more often recognized as authorities in their fields. By confidently asserting your expertise, leveraging your knowledge, and actively seeking opportunities to showcase your skills, you can triumph over gender barriers. Building a robust professional network and continuously advocating for your contributions will further solidify your position as a leader in your field. Empowerment and progress are on the rise!

My Journey to Becoming an Expert

My path to expertise was anything but linear—it was filled with obstacles and moments of self-doubt. Entering the tech industry straight out of college with a history degree, I was ill-equipped to compete with men armed with engineering degrees. The odds were against me, and the environment was often intimidating. However, I refused to let these challenges hinder my growth and pursued every opportunity to learn and develop my skills.

I asked and received training from experienced professionals who were willing to guide me in my career. These efforts paid off when I started as an Account Executive and rose to Senior Executive roles. I often found myself as one of the few women in male-dominated companies and industries. By confidently positioning myself as an expert-in-training in sales and leadership, I broke through barriers, won numerous awards, and gained the respect of my colleagues and superiors. These challenging situations helped me build relationships and create advocates, allies, and strategic partners with men in highly competitive industries.

Today, I stand as a testament to the power of perseverance and self-belief. I am committed to helping other women navigate their paths to expertise, empowering them to break through barriers and achieve their full potential. Remember, your journey might be tough, but the rewards of unwaveringly positioning yourself as a leader are invaluable.

Strategies for Overcoming Obstacles

To transcend these obstacles and fully express your expertise, adopt a proactive and resilient mindset. Embrace challenges as opportunities for growth and remain persistent in the face of setbacks. Cultivate a continuous learning habit and seek out new experiences that push your boundaries. Hire a great coach whom you admire. There's nothing that compares to getting personalized support and mentorship. Surround yourself with a supportive network of mentors and peers who can provide guidance and encouragement. Here are key strategies to bolster your journey to expertise:

Practice Self-Affirmation

Regularly affirm your achievements and expertise. Take time to meticulously document your successes and positive feedback, perhaps in a journal or a digital app. Reflect on these accomplishments frequently to strengthen self-belief and remind yourself of your capabilities. This practice boosts confidence and provides a tangible record of your growth and progress over time.

Advocacy

Advocate for yourself and other women by actively promoting inclusivity and recognition within your industry. Speak up in meetings, support women's voices and achievements, and mentor those newer to the field. Challenge biases whenever they arise and work toward creating an environment that values and respects diverse expertise. By fostering a culture of mutual support and respect, we can pave the way for more equitable opportunities and a more inclusive professional community.

Mentorship and Support Networks

Engage with mentors and supportive networks, such as the C-Suite Network Women's Coaching & Consulting Council, which are specifically designed to promote and showcase women coaches and consultants. These platforms provide invaluable guidance, resources, and encouragement, fostering a community of shared growth and empowerment. Through interactive live streams, one-on-one coaching, and networking events, members gain insights from experienced professionals, share their challenges and opportunities, and celebrate their successes together.

How To Expand Your Expertise

- **Pursue Visibility And Recognition:** Actively seek opportunities to showcase your expertise across various platforms. Consider speaking at industry conferences to present your insights and engage with peers. Join panel discussions to offer your unique perspective and network with other experts. These activities validate your expertise and enhance your visibility and credibility in your field.

- **Commit to Continuous Learning:** Becoming an expert is an ongoing journey. Maintain a thirst for knowledge, stay abreast of industry trends, and constantly seek ways to refine your skills. Attend conferences for new insights and networking, take courses to deepen your expertise, read thought-provoking books, listen to insightful podcasts, and learn from successful experts in your field.

- **Cultivate Your Network:** Build a robust network of like-minded individuals and experts to foster collaboration and learning opportunities. Attend industry events, join professional groups, and engage in online communities to connect with others. These relationships can offer valuable insights, support, and potential partnerships that can propel your career or business forward.

The Role of Coaching and Mentorship

Becoming a founding member of the C-Suite Network Women's Coaching & Consulting Council is a decisive step toward harnessing your full potential. This council offers a robust platform for collaboration, learning, and support among like-minded women leaders. The importance of having a coach or mentor cannot be overstated. Specially trained coaches provide personalized guidance, challenge us to reach higher, and offer valuable feedback that sharpens our edge.

Mentors share their experiences and wisdom, helping us navigate complex professional landscapes. They illuminate paths that might otherwise remain unseen and provide the moral support needed to overcome setbacks. Both coaches and mentors play pivotal roles in our professional journeys, acting as catalysts that expedite our growth and enhance our impact.

Conclusion

Your expertise, passion, and dedication are your greatest assets. By confidently establishing yourself as an authority in your field, you advance your career and inspire and empower others. Being recognized as a knowledgeable and influential professional can open doors to new opportunities and collaborations that might otherwise remain out of reach. Remember, it's not just about what you know; it's about how you use that knowledge to make a tangible difference in your industry and community.

Ready to take the next step in your expert journey? Book a consultation to map out your path to becoming an industry-leading expert and thought leader. During this session, we'll dive deep into your goals, current achievements, and the strategies you can implement to reach new heights. Whether you're looking to increase your income, expand your influence, publish thought-provoking content, or engage with more corporate clients, we have the tools and insights to guide you.

By following these steps and strategies, you'll be well on your way to achieving greater success and significance in your career. Let's break through barriers together and redefine what it means to be an expert in today's world. With dedication and the right approach, you can set new standards of excellence and be a source of inspiration for your peers. So, take that bold step forward, and let's embark on this transformative journey together.

Author Bio

Kathleen Caldwell

Kathleen Caldwell is an Advanced Clinical Hypnotherapist and Certified Corporate Coach. She is founder of C-Suite Network's Women's Coaching & Consulting Council™ and the Women's Success Accelerator™, designed to mentor women coaches, consultants, trusted advisors, experts, and thought leaders in creating six- and seven-figure businesses through group coaching, councils, and corporate coaching offers. She also leads Caldwell Consulting Group, LLC.™, a consultancy specializing in business strategy and peak performance. CCG guides clients to enhanced leadership, increased profitability, and unparallelled thought and market leadership. Their services include strategy planning, consulting, coaching, keynote speaking, workshops, and programs such as Team Intelligence® and Increasing Your Influence, Income, and Impact™.

Kathleen has received numerous awards and honors including the designation of "Woman of Distinction" and "Influential Woman in Business" and was recently honored as a GEM – Generous, Enthusiastic and Motivated leader in her community.

Awards, aside, Ms. Caldwell is known best as a philanthropist, global people connector and is excited to share her alliances and new business strategies to support leaders and organizations in their business and career success. Drawing from decades of corporate leadership experience in technology, Kathleen stands for a world where all women are "Seen. Heard And Richly Rewarded™."

In her spare time, Kathleen is a certified Zumba instructor, health coach, and success hypnotherapist and has a passion for international travel and ballroom dancing with her sweetheart and husband, Michael.

- linkedin.com/in/kathleencaldwellcoach/

I dedicate this chapter to all who have contributed to my journey in my wonderful life. Through the mountains climbed, the valleys overcome, the lessons learned, the sadness felt, and the joy experienced, I thank you.

Leaning Into My Journey: Relearning to Achieve My Dreams

Michelle Beauchamp

Breast cancer walks have been a significant part of my life for the past ten years. They have ignited my passion for transforming leadership in business and community. My journey has led me to walk alongside survivors, tirelessly raise funds, and witness firsthand the impact of grit and tenacity on women's leadership. This experience has taught me the power of resilience, determination, and the strength that comes from standing together for a common cause.

My personal experiences of perseverance and determination include leading a team representing Oprah, raising $100k, and overcoming challenges in my entrepreneurial journey. I learned many lessons from walking in breast cancer walks, leaving a secure leadership job to start a business, running a successful venture for over five years, and eventually documenting my experiences in my first book, "Relearn Leadership."

One overarching lesson I learned is that grit and tenacity can transform women's leadership journeys. Years ago, I created an acronym, GRIT, to reinforce the value of achievement. I'm happy to share it below:

Gratitude- I am always mindful to be grateful for my past, present, and future. My past has led me to where I am today; my present is shaping me into who I will become, and my future holds endless possibilities for me to make a positive impact on the lives of others.

Resilience- I understand that obstacles are a part of life, and it's essential to be able to bounce back and keep moving forward.

Integrity- My authenticity lies in pursuing my passion, being with like-minded people, and not conforming to others' values or standards.

Tenacity- My self-talk involves summoning the courage to venture beyond my comfort zone and embrace the greatness that awaits me.

Walking in Breast Cancer Walks: A Journey in Empathy and Advocacy

During my first year of walking, I observed people continuing to walk despite their aching muscles, bandaged knees, and blistered feet. The lesson that I learned from witnessing this pain and carried with me in all my subsequent walks was to push through the pain. In other words, having grit and determination will enable you to persevere.

For the third year, I decided to walk in San Francisco, a departure from my two previous walks in Santa Barbara. It was time for me to become courageous and tenacious and overcome my fear of bridges over bodies of water. I knew that they walked across the bridge in this walk, and I was ready to conquer fear. As we approached the bridge, I became nervous, but the person I was walking with, Sandy, encouraged me and spoke words of affirmation to me. I did it! The most exciting part was when we crossed the bridge again on day two. I was calm and knew that I had conquered that fear. I was filled with gratitude!

During the walk, soon after we crossed the bridge on day one, a photographer asked if he could take my photo. I signed several release statements, he gave me different shoes for the New Balance sponsor, and I took several poses. This photo generated so much excitement and pride because it showed up as a full-page ad in Oprah Magazine three times. It was in subway stations and point-of-sale items in all the seven cities where the walk occurred! What a fun experience. During this time, my youngest son attended college in Santa Barbara, one of the seven locations of the walk. He was in a restaurant with a buddy, and I was there, in a table tent. He was so excited and told his buddy the picture was his mom. The buddy didn't believe him so he called me to prove it. Reflecting on this still makes me smile and is another example of gratitude. This story describes how this experience impacted my community leadership.

On the opposite page of my photo was a full-page advertisement seeking team captains in four cities (one of which was Santa Barbara, where I planned to walk) to represent Oprah Magazine. As soon as I saw it, I became interested and wondered if I could take on such a challenge. My inner voice assured me that I could, so I applied, and to my delight, I was accepted.

To summarize, I led Team O for two consecutive years, and we raised $100,000 (the highest volume of the four city teams)! This experience helped me to apply the leadership skills I had developed at work and a sense of integrity and alignment. For instance, leaders are responsible for painting the picture and sharing the vision. I created a vision to have at least 20 people on our team, and in year one, we had 21 team members, and in year two, we had 20 walkers. Walking 39.3 miles was a challenge that none of us had ever faced. However, I instilled a belief in our team that if they trained consistently and followed the guidelines provided to us, they would be able to achieve it.

Fundraising can be daunting for most people, as asking for money is difficult. I helped them shift their mindset and understand that they were not asking for money for themselves but for a noble cause to impact the lives of others. I also offered some scripts to use as they wrote emails, made calls, and sent letters and texts. They practiced tenacity.

The influx of donations brought them immense joy and a sense of purpose. As they walked through the hills of Santa Barbara, they forged a deep bond, creating memories that would last a lifetime. I hope this event continues to hold the same significance for them as it does for me. May they carry the same enthusiasm, persistence, and grit in their hearts as they face similar challenges in the future.

Leaving a Secure Leadership Position: Embracing Entrepreneurship

You've heard the term "golden handcuffs," right? In case you haven't, it means yearning to branch out and leave the high salary plus bonus, benefits, and automatic vacation—in other words, security but being fearful to step out of your comfort zone.

I have attempted previous businesses, but I could not sustain them due to reasons like inadequate capital or economic downturns. However, I believed that if I could have one more chance to start and build a business, I could achieve success. This desire came from deep within my heart and soul.

For three years, my vision board showed a picture of a person jumping from one hill to another with the giant words Leap of Faith next to the photo. I was so glad to finally be able to remove it when I leaped to leave my corporate position and launch my new business.

Having a solid support system is essential. My husband always supported my desire for another chance, but we knew we had to be innovative. In September 2018, I retired to rewire. By April 2020, I had achieved great clarity about my goals. I had built strong relationships, resulting in my biggest month ever in business revenue. But we know what happened in March 2020: COVID-19. Everything changed except for my passion and commitment to building a business.

Did I like having to experience disappointment, lose business, and start over? NO! The community and country shared the same commonality, and I think everyone recognized the critical need to shift. We proved that we are resilient people. Upon wondering what to do, I was fortunate to utilize some resources in the John Maxwell program, in which I was certified. I received good ideas and encouragement. Like almost everyone else, I learned that technology was my new friend, and I could conduct meetings and training virtually. Now, I appreciate the efficiency of these meetings and the effectiveness and collaboration potential through virtual training.

I value building relationships through networking and connecting with others. I struggled with networking virtually because I was used to the human touch. Now, though, I am mastering the skill of virtual networking and appreciating the value of using LinkedIn.

Learning Through Lessons of Challenge and Success

I am a lifelong learner and am inspired to keep growing. To become my best self, I continue to jump on webinars, register for classes, read books and articles, and listen to podcasts. This is where tenacity and resilience come in. As an entrepreneur, I value boldness and creativity. I understand things as the mist has cleared, and I can see everything.

But, just as quickly as it disappeared, the fog rolled over again like a cloud over a mountain, shrouding everything in uncertainty and leaving me searching for clarity once more. The poster on the office wall in front of me says, "A possibility thinker believes there is always an answer," by John Maxwell, reminding me to persist and think outside the box.

I am a spirit-filled woman, and I often review 2 Timothy verse 1:7: "For God did not give us a spirit of timidity, but a spirit of power, of love, and of self-discipline."

First, look within...

I constantly evaluate my mindset. One of the items on my vision board, which I look at daily, asks, "What are you Thinking?" I must admit that when I reflect, I sometimes have some stinking thinking. So, I reset and look for the positive, and my behaviors follow.

Another item on my vision board is a bridge with a lemon, a glass of lemonade, and the statement, "Find A Way." This motivates me to believe in my mission, keep pushing forward, and provide more inspiration to remain resilient.

Self-awareness and confidence building are at the core of my training. Success is an inside job, and it begins within. I encourage people to write and repeat affirmations out loud. Some participants feel this is kind of a woo-woo exercise, but once saying the affirmations become a habit, they acknowledge that their confidence increases, and they have more impact.

If we build it, they will come...

I attended a marketing workshop during a coaches' and trainers' conference. The instructor informed us that coaching and training were not our business. He continued to tell us that, in fact, we were in the marketing business.

That comment threw me off for a while, and I wondered what he meant. A few months later, I finally understood. Even though I had a coaching and training business, I needed a consistent and targeted marketing strategy to establish myself as a thought leader. This would enable potential clients to find me and seek my services.

When I started my current business, The Champ Group, I was surprised by the amount of marketing required compared to when I had my business ten years prior. Back then, I could attend networking events, participate in committees, develop relationships, and receive referrals. However, I quickly discovered the power of social media. I am still adjusting to the need to stay consistent with posting relevant material, staying in touch with people, and scheduling various meetings to get acquainted. It's important to be willing to adapt to new changes and trends in the industry.

I wanted to add value to others, so three years ago, I started my monthly program, Champ Chat. In it, I invite others to join me in conversations on topics related to people and culture. It's proven to be an excellent way to meet new people and establish my reputation as a thought leader. Plus, it allows the guest speakers to receive publicity to expand their thought leader reputation and transform their business. A crucial leadership attribute is reciprocity, and I have discovered that this program empowers me to help others succeed.

Spreading My Message by Becoming an Author

Writing my first book in 2023 was a true testament to my grit and tenacity. It aligns perfectly with my philosophy of setting goals and seeing them through until the end. To accomplish this, I had to practice the same skills I teach others, like discipline, mindset, consistency, planning, and knowing one's why. It was a challenging yet rewarding experience that taught me much about perseverance and dedication. I saw the book as an opportunity to help others grow, and I recognize that when we are willing to step out of our comfort zones and trust that we can be adaptable, we can positively affect others.

Another important reminder was the benefit of partnership and collaboration. I used to perceive people who did similar work to what I did as competitors. I later understood that that perception was one of scarcity, which didn't align with my values or principles. Through my journey of personal development and my commitment to lifelong learning, I have realized that changing our mindset to abundance can significantly impact our lives. By focusing on abundance, we can recognize that there is enough for everyone and that success is not a zero-sum game. This shift in mindset has allowed me to approach challenges with a more positive outlook and has opened new opportunities that I never thought were possible before. My experiences have given me experience, knowledge, and wisdom. And it's so refreshing to engage with others to gather the thoughts and perspectives their experiences have generated and learn from them.

I feel blessed to have had so many unique experiences, celebrated so many wonderful achievements, and overcome so many obstacles. I am ready to enjoy the greatness the future will bring. In this chapter, I leaned on my journey, relearning to achieve my dreams and inspiring you to go and get your blessings!

Author Bio

Michelle Beauchamp

Michelle's passion is, quite simply, helping people grow. Her motto, "Unleash Your Inner Champ," is evident in her client relationship rapport, vast course curriculum, design structure, and delivery method.

Michelle's commitment to personal and professional development is unwavering. As a certified coach, speaker, and trainer on the John Maxwell Team, she embodies this commitment, striving for leadership excellence in all her endeavors.

Michelle's 25 years in Corporate America as a Sales
Leader in Telecommunications, combined with her 15 + years as an entrepreneur, has equipped her to help others explore their strengths, improve areas of weakness and through a journey of inner discovery, create and lead inclusive cultures that enrich relationships and increase productivity.

Michelle is not just a trainer, but a skilled one who designs Leadership development courses that provide a comprehensive understanding of the content and practical activities. Her approach, which encourages participants to apply the lessons presented, has proven to be highly effective in boosting confidence and competence, and facilitating a smooth transition from the classroom to the real world.

The community she leads, EmpowerHer Collective, empowers women to embrace their talents and ambitions and achieve their potential through collaboration, continuous learning, and connection. Michelle believes that leadership begins within, and until we commit to developing ourselves, we cannot gain and keep the trust of others we influence.

- thechampgroup.com
- linkedin.com/in/MichelleBeauchamp

Manufactured by Amazon.ca
Acheson, AB

15360675R00105